BRIGHT NOTES

CORIOLANUS BY WILLIAM SHAKESPEARE

Intelligent Education

Nashville, Tennessee

BRIGHT NOTES: Coriolanus
www.BrightNotes.com

ISBN: 978-1-645425-56-4 (Paperback)
ISBN: 978-1-645425-57-1 (eBook)

Published in accordance with the U.S. Copyright Office Orphan Works and Mass Digitization report of the register of copyrights, June 2015.

Originally published by Monarch Press.
Margaret Loftus Ranald, 1966
2020 Edition published by Influence Publishers.

Interior design by Lapiz Digital Services. Cover Design by Thinkpen Designs.

Printed in the United States of America.

Library of Congress Cataloging-in-Publication Data forthcoming.
Names: Intelligent Education
Title: BRIGHT NOTES: Coriolanus
Subject: STU004000 STUDY AIDS / Book Notes

CONTENTS

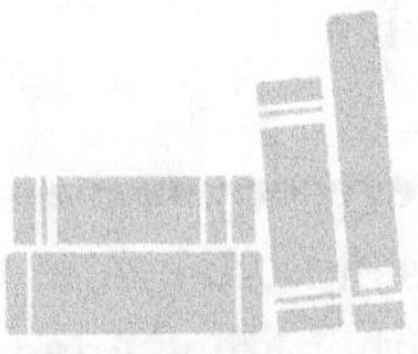

INTRODUCTION TO WILLIAM SHAKESPEARE

FACTS VERSUS SPECULATION

Anyone who wishes to know where documented truth ends and where speculation begins in Shakespearean scholarship and criticism first needs to know the facts of Shakespeare's life. A medley of life records suggest, by their lack of inwardness, how little is known of Shakespeare's ideology, his beliefs and opinions.

William Shakespeare was baptized on April 26, 1564, as "Gulielmus filius Johannes Shakespeare"; the evidence is the parish register of Holy Trinity Church, Stratford, England.

HUSBAND AND FATHER

On November 28, 1582, the Bishop of Worcester issued a license to William Shakespeare and "Anne Hathaway of Stratford" to solemnize a marriage upon one asking of the banns providing that there were no legal impediments. Three askings of the banns were (and are) usual in the Church of England.

On May 26, 1583, the records of the parish church in Stratford note the baptism of Susanna, daughter to William Shakespeare. The inference is clear, then, that Anne Hathaway Shakespeare was with child at the time of her wedding.

On February 2, 1585, the records of the parish church in Stratford note the baptisms of "Hamnet & Judeth, sonne and daughter to William Shakespeare."

SHAKESPEARE INSULTED

On September 20, 1592, Robert Greene's A Groats-worth of witte, bought with a million of Repentance was entered in the Stationers' Register. In this work Shakespeare was publicly insulted as "an upstart Crow, beautified with our ["gentlemen" playwrights usually identified as Marlowe, Nashe, and Lodge] feathers, that with Tygers hart wrapt in a Players hyde [a **parody** of a Shakespearean line in II Henry VI] supposes he is as well able to bombast out a **blank verse** as the best of you: and being an absolute Johannes factotum, is in his own conceit the only Shake-scene in a country." This statement asperses not only Shakespeare's art but intimates his base, i.e., non-gentle, birth. A "John factotum" is a servant or a man of all work.

On April 18, 1593, Shakespeare's long erotic poem *Venus and Adonis* was entered for publication. It was printed under the author's name and was dedicated to the nineteen-year-old Henry Wriothesley, Earl of Southampton.

On May 9, 1594, another long erotic poem, *The Rape of Lucrece,* was entered for publication. It also was printed under Shakespeare's name and was dedicated to the Earl of Southampton.

On December 26 and 27, 1594, payment was made to Shakespeare and others for performances at court by the Lord Chamberlain's servants.

For August 11, 1596, the parish register of Holy Trinity Church records the burial of "Hamnet filius William Shakespeare."

FROM "VILLEIN" TO "GENTLEMAN"

On October 20, 1596, John Shakespeare, the poet's father, was made a "gentleman" by being granted the privilege of bearing a coat of arms. Thus, William Shakespeare on this day also became a "gentleman." Shakespeare's mother, Mary Arden Shakespeare, was "gentle" by birth. The poet was a product of a cross-class marriage. Both the father and the son were technically "villeins" or "villains" until this day.

On May 24, 1597, William Shakespeare purchased New Place, a large house in the center of Stratford.

CITED AS "BEST"

In 1598 Francis Meres's Palladis Tamia listed Shakespeare more frequently than any other English author. Shakespeare was cited as one of eight by whom "the English tongue is mightily enriched, and gorgeouslie invested in rare ornaments and resplendent abiliments"; as one of six who had raised monumentum aere perennius [a monument more lasting than brass]; as one of five who excelled in lyric poetry; as one of thirteen "best for Tragedie," and as one of seventeen who were "best for Comedy."

On September 20, 1598, Shakespeare is said on the authority of Ben Jonson (in his collection of plays, 1616) to have been an actor in Jonson's *Every Man in His Humour*.

On September 8, 1601, the parish register of Holy Trinity in Stratford records the burial of "Mr. Johannes Shakespeare," the poet's father.

BECOMES A "KING'S MAN"

In 1603 Shakespeare was named among others, the Lord Chamberlain's players, as licensed by James I (Queen Elizabeth having died) to become the King's Men.

In 1603 a garbled and pirated *Hamlet* (now known as *Q1*) was printed with Shakespeare's name on the title page.

In March 1604, King James gave Shakespeare, as one of the Grooms of the Chamber (by virtue of being one of the King's Men), four yards of red cloth for a livery, this being in connection with a royal progress through the City of London.

In 1604 (probably) there appeared a second version of *Hamlet* (now known as *Q2*), enlarged and corrected, with Shakespeare's name on the title page.

On June 5, 1607, the parish register at Stratford records the marriage of "M. John Hall gentleman & Susanna Shakespeare," the poet's elder daughter. John Hall was a doctor of medicine.

BECOMES A GRANDFATHER

On February 21, 1608, the parish register at Holy Trinity, Stratford, records the baptism of Elizabeth Hall, Shakespeare's first grandchild.

On September 9, 1608, the parish register at Holy Trinity, Stratford, records the burial of Mary Shakespeare, the poet's mother.

On May 20, 1609, "Shakespeares Sonnets. Never before Imprinted" was entered for publication.

On February 10, 1616, the marriage of Judith, Shakespeare's younger daughter, is recorded in the parish register of Holy Trinity, Stratford.

On March 25, 1616, Shakespeare made his will. It is extant.

On April 23, 1616, Shakespeare died. The monument in the Stratford church is authority for the date.

BURIED IN STRATFORD CHURCH

On April 25, 1616, Shakespeare was buried in Holy Trinity Church, Stratford. Evidence of this date is found in the church register. A stone laid over his grave bears the inscription:

Good Frend for Jesus Sake Forbeare, To Digg The Dust Encloased Heare! Blest Be Ye Man Yt Spares Thes Stones, And Curst Be He Yt Moves My Bones.

DEMAND FOR MORE INFORMATION

These are the life records of Shakespeare. Biographers, intent on book length or even short accounts of the life of the poet, of necessity flesh out these (and other) not very revealing notices from 1564-1616, Shakespeare's life span with ancillary matter such as the status of Elizabethan actors, details of the Elizabethan theaters, and life under Elizabeth I and James I. Information about Shakespeare's artistic life-for example, his alteration of his sources-is much more abundant than truthful insights into his personal life, including his beliefs. There is, of course, great demand for colorful stories about Shakespeare, and there is intense pressure on biographers to depict the poet as a paragon of wisdom.

ANECDOTES-TRUE OR UNTRUE?

Biographers of Shakespeare may include stories about Shakespeare that have been circulating since at least the seventeenth century; no one knows whether or not these stories are true. One declares that Shakespeare was an apprentice to a butcher, that he ran away from his master, and was received by actors in London. Another story holds that Shakespeare was, in his youth, a schoolmaster somewhere in the country. Another story has Shakespeare fleeing from his native town to escape the clutches of Sir Thomas Lucy who had often had him whipped and sometimes imprisoned for poaching deer. Yet another story represents the youthful Shakespeare as holding horses and taking care of them while their owners attended the theater. And there are other stories.

Scholarly and certainly lay expectations oblige Shakespearean biographers often to resort to speculation. This may be very well if biographers use such words as conjecture, presumably, seems, and almost certainly. I quote an example of this kind of hedged thought and language from Hazelton Spencer's *The Art and Life of William Shakespeare* (1940); "Of politics Shakespeare seems to have steered clear ... but at least by implication Shakespeare reportedly endorses the strong-monarchy policy of the Tudors and Stuarts." Or one may say, as I do in my book *Blood Will Tell in Shakespeare's Plays* (1984): "Shakespeare particularly faults his numerous villeins for lacking the classical virtue of courage (they are cowards) and for deficiencies in reasoning ability (they are 'fools'), and in speech (they commit malapropisms), for lack of charity, for ambition, for unsightly faces and poor physiques, for their smell, and for their harboring lice." This remark is not necessarily biographical or reflective of Shakespeare's personal beliefs; it refers to Shakespeare's art in that it makes general assertions about the base - those who lacked coats of arms-as they appear in the poet's thirty-seven plays. The remark's truth or lack of truth may be tested by examination of Shakespeare's writings.

WHO WROTE SHAKESPEARE'S PLAYS?

The less reputable biographers of Shakespeare, including some of weighty names, state assumptions as if they were facts concerning the poet's beliefs. Perhaps the most egregious are those who cannot conceive that the Shakespearean plays were written by a person not a graduate of Oxford or Cambridge and destitute of the insights permitted by foreign travel and by life at court. Those of this persuasion insist that the seventeenth Earl of Oxford, Edward de Vere (whose descendant Charles Vere recently spoke up for the Earl's authorship of the Shakespearean plays), or Sir Francis Bacon, or someone else wrote the Shakespearean plays. It is also argued that the stigma of publication would besmirch the honor of an Elizabethan gentleman who published under his own name (unless he could pretend to correct a pirated printing of his writings).

BEN JONSON KNEW HIM WELL

Suffice it here to say that the thought of anyone writing the plays and giving them to the world in the name of Shakespeare would have astonished Ben Jonson, a friend of the poet, who literally praised Shakespeare to the skies for his comedies and tragedies in the fine poem "To the Memory of My Beloved Master the Author, Mr. William Shakespeare, and What He Hath Left Us" (printed in the *First Folio*, 1623). Much more commonplace and therefore much more obtrusive upon the minds of Shakespeare students are those many scholars who are capable of writing, for example, that Shakespeare put more of himself into Hamlet than any of his other characters or that the poet had no rigid system of religion or morality. Even George Lyman Kittredge, the greatest American Shakespearean, wrote, "Hamlet's advice to the players has always been understood - and rightly - to embody Shakespeare's own views on the art of acting."

In point of fact, we know nothing of Shakespeare's beliefs or opinions except such obvious inferences as that he must have thought New Place, Stratford, worth buying because he bought it. Even Homer, a very self-effacing poet, differs in this matter from Shakespeare. Twice in the Iliad he speaks in his own voice (distinguished from the dialogue of his characters) about certain evil deeds of Achilles. Shakespeare left no letters, no diary, and no prefaces (not counting conventionally obsequious dedications); no Elizabethan Boswell tagged Shakespeare around London and the provinces to record his conversation and thus to reveal his mind. In his plays Shakespeare employed no rainsonneur, or authorial mouthpiece, as some other dramatists have done: contrary to many scholarly assertions, it cannot be proved that Prospero, in *The Tempest* in the speech ending "I'll drown my book" (Act V), and *Ulysses*, in *Troilus and Cressida* in the long speech on "degree" (Act II), speak Shakespeare's own sentiments. All characters in all Shakespearean plays speak for themselves. Whether they speak also for Shakespeare cannot be proved because documents outside the plays cannot be produced.

As for the sonnets, they have long been the happy hunting ground of biographical crackpots who lack outside documents, who do not recognize that Shakespeare may have been using a persona, and who seem not to know that in Shakespeare's time good **sonnets** were supposed to read like confessions.

Some critics even go to the length of professing to hear Shakespeare speaking in the speech of a character and uttering his private beliefs. An example may be found in A. L. Rowse's *What Shakespeare Read and Thought* (1981): "Nor is it so difficult to know what Shakespeare thought or felt. A writer, Logan Pearsall Smith, had the perception to see that a personal tone of voice enters when Shakespeare is telling you what he thinks, sometimes almost a raised voice; it is more obvious again when he urges the same point over and over."

BUT THERE'S NO PROOF!

Rowse, deeply enamoured of his ability to hear Shakespeare's own thoughts in the speeches of characters speaking in character, published a volume entitled *Shakespeare's Self-Portrait, Passages from His Work* (1984). One critic might hear Shakespeare voicing his own thoughts in a speech in *Hamlet*; another might hear the author in *Macbeth*. Shakespearean writings can become a vast whispering gallery where Shakespeare himself is heard hic et ubique (here and everywhere), without an atom of documentary proof.

"BETTER SO"

Closer to truth is Matthew Arnold's poem on Shakespeare:

Others abide our question. Thou art free. We ask and ask - thou smilest and art still, Out-topping knowledge. For the loftiest hill, Who to the stars uncrowns his majesty, Planting his steadfast footsteps in the sea, Making the heaven of heavens his dwelling Spares but the cloudy border of his base To the foiled searching of mortality; And thou, who didst the stars and sunbeams know, Self-schooled, self-scanned, self-honored, self-secure, Didst tread the earth unguessed at. - Better so....

Here Arnold has Dichtung und Wahrheit - both poetry and truth - with at least two abatements: he exaggerates Shakespeare's wisdom - the poet, after all, is not God; and Arnold fails to acknowledge that Shakespeare's genius was variously recognized in his own time. Jonson, for example, recorded that the "players [actors of the poet's time] have often mentioned it as an honor to Shakespeare, that in his writing (whatsoever he penned) he never blotted a line" (*Timber*), and of course there is praise of Shakespeare, some of it quoted above, in Meres's *Palladis Tamia* (1598).

THE BEST APPROACH

Hippocrates' first apothegm states, "Art is long, but life is short." Even Solomon complained of too many books. One must be, certainly in our time, very selective. Shakespeare's ipsissima verba (his very words) should of course be studied, and some of them memorized. Then, if one has time, the golden insights of criticism from the eighteenth century to the present should be perused. (The problem is to find them all in one book!) And the vast repetitiousness, the jejune stating of the obvious, and the rampant subjectivity of much Shakespearean criticism should be shunned.

Then, if time serves, the primary sources of Shakespeare's era should be studied because the plays were not impervious to colorings imparted by the historical matrix. Finally, if the exigencies of life permit, biographers of Shakespeare who distinguish between fact and guesswork, such as Marchette Chute (*Shakespeare of London*), should be consulted. The happiest situation, pointed to by Jesus in Milton's *Paradise Regained*, is to bring judgment informed by knowledge to whatever one reads.

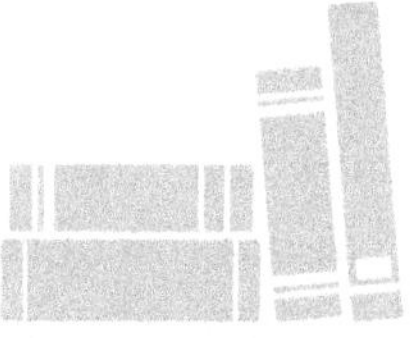

CORIOLANUS

INTRODUCTION

GENERAL

This play has not always been a popular one, but in recent years it has been attracting more notice and more study. Part of the difficulty with it has been its intense intellectuality, and what some critics have considered its extremely "Roman" and austere tone. This coldness is particularly marked when one compares *Coriolanus* with the other tragedies, particularly with its nearest counterpart among the Roman plays, *Antony and Cleopatra*, which is noted for the sheer gorgeousness of its property. By contrast, *Coriolanus* is a fine example of Shakespeare's late, lean, and compact style in which images are used for their intellectual and thematic import, rather than their emotional content. Lastly, the character of the hero seems at first glance to be unsympathetic, and at times even repellent in his attitudes. Nevertheless, the play is almost invariably successful on the stage today, particularly in the recent performances of Sir Laurence Olivier, Richard Burton, and Paul Scofield. In addition, modern scholarship and the political events of the twentieth century have disclosed new meanings and new timeliness in this play.

THE SOURCES

The major source for *Coriolanus* is the "Life of Caius Marcius" in Plutarch's *Lives of the Noble Grecians and Romans*. This account of Greek and Roman political worthies was translated first into French by Jacques Amyot. In 1579, it was turned into a superb English translation, by Sir Thomas North, which was frequently reprinted. It was the North translation that Shakespeare used as the foundation for the events detailed in this play. In addition, he seems to have used William Camden's *Remaines of a Greater Work Concerning Britaine* (1605) for some aspects of Menenius' tale of the belly and the members.

On the whole Shakespeare follows his major source, North's *Plutarch*, fairly closely, but as is usual with him, he has made some changes in his material. The greatest change, of course, is one of compression for dramatic purposes. Shakespeare reduces the separate commotions of the people to two, the corn riot and the banishment riot. In *Plutarch* the first, which concluded with the appointment of the Tribunes, actually took place in 494 B.C. and was apparently pacified by Menenius. The second, which was totally omitted by Shakespeare, arose over an alleged plot by the patricians, the nobles, to thin out the ranks of the discontented plebeians, the common people, by drafting them into the army. It was after this rebellion in Plutarch that *Coriolanus* was offered the consulship, only to have it refused him, despite his having returned to Rome with food and the spoils of war. Following on this refusal, a third tumult when *Coriolanus* refused to give corn to the populace. As a result *Coriolanus* was banished. By combining these three commotions in Act I, Shakespeare makes the banishment almost a separate issue, and plays down the participation of the tribunes by omitting the second rebellion. More emphasis is given to the legitimate grievances of the people, but considerable stress is laid on the fickleness and general ignorance of the crowd.

Shakespeare has created something unique in the central character of *Coriolanus*, and also in that of his mother. Coriolanus in Plutarch is said to have been lacking in education because he had been brought up by his mother, Volumnia. In Shakespeare we have an unusually well portrayed mature female character, and the relationship between mother and son is made extremely important for the course of the play. In Plutarch, too, Valeria is the guiding spirit behind the ladies' visit to Coriolanus among the Volscians, whereas in Shakespeare Volumnia is responsible. This change emphasizes the importance of the mother-son relationship and gives added motivation to *Coriolanus*. As for Coriolanus, himself, Shakespeare has been unusually objective. He has shown the worst side of his hero as well as his best in his military and family relationships, at times even running the risk of alienating our sympathies from the hero. Finally, Shakespeare has really invented the character of Menenius Agrippa, the "humorous patrician," from a few hints in much the same way as he created the loyal old soldier Enobarbus in *Antony and Cleopatra*. Significantly, Menenius is the nearest approach to a comic character in the entire play. Shakespeare also alters the character of Aufidius, showing us more of him, and making him even more of a foil to *Coriolanus*.

The major **theme** of the Plutarch source is also shifted in the play's continual emphasis on the personality of Coriolanus. Whereas the Roman writer was more concerned with ethics and politics, Shakespeare stressed the development of character intertwined with the **theme** of politics. As a result, the play contains a central personality who dominates the play, and whose tragedy is both personal and political.

HISTORICAL BACKGROUND

The city of Rome was founded in 753 B.C. by the legendary twins Romulus and Remus, and Roman events were counted from that date for the founding of the city, or A. U. C., Ab Urbe Condita. The early history of the city is lost in legend, but for a time it was ruled by kings. In 510 B.C. the Romans, tired of the tyranny of the rulers, the Tarquins, drove them out and set up a republic with two Consuls as rulers. They had the powers of a King, but they were chosen for a term of one year only. The Senate, a council of the heads of noble families, acted in an advisory capacity to the Consuls. In time of severe national danger a Dictator, usually a man of some military experience, could be appointed as supreme head of state for a period of six months, or the duration of the national emergency.

There were in Rome two separate classes, the Patricians and the Plebeians. The former were nobles and could send representatives to the Senate. The latter, the common people, suffered political, economic, and social disabilities and could not aspire to membership in the Senate or to the office of magistrate. In 494 B.C., after a military mutiny, the Plebeians were given two Tribunes as representatives. The Tribunes were charged with looking after the interests of the common people, and if they thought a Plebeian was being sentenced unjustly they had the right to say "I forbid," in Latin, "Veto." Class hatred persisted between the Patricians and Plebeians, and about twenty years after the events of this play the Plebeians managed to gain some semblance of free voting for their Tribunes and therefore some real political power. The events of the play *Coriolanus* cover about four years, 491 B.C. to 487 B.C., though historically the battle at Corioli took place in 493 B.C.

TEXT AND DATE

The play first appeared in the First Folio of 1623, and the text is not very satisfactory, chiefly because of mislineations. In addition, because of the closely packed and almost cryptic style, verbal corruptions are hard to correct, as also are other errors. Since the stage directions are unusually full, noting gesture and position on the stage, textual critics have suggested that they were written by Shakespeare.

There is little definite external evidence concerning the date, and in general much of what is offered is a trifle questionable. A reference to ripe mulberries in III.ii is thought to refer to James I's instructions in 1609 to encourage their growth, but the fruit was known in England before then. There was a dearth of corn in England and a consequent insurrection in the Midlands in 1608-9, but Plutarch includes a dearth, and there was another peasant uprising in Northamptonshire, this one against enclosures, the fencing off of common land. Possibly "coals of fire upon the ice," may refer to the disastrous frost of 1607-8 during which the Thames froze over and fires were built on it. But, as E. K. Chambers points out, Shakespeare may have seen this phenomenon an another, smaller river. Some suggestion has been made that the character of Volumnia arises from Shakespeare's recollection of what he himself owed to his mother, who was buried on September 9, 1608. However, one wonders whether the attributes of the staunch Roman matron would constitute a compliment to a dead mother. Other scholars have seen some aspects of Sir Walter Ralegh in Coriolanus himself, and some treatment of the struggles of King James I and his refractory parliaments. None of these pieces of external evidence is very satisfactory, and evidence drawn from the study of style and meter places the play fairly late. Chambers suggests 1607-1608, but certainly after *Antony and Cleopatra* and before the last plays.

POETRY AND IMAGERY

The poetic style of this play is characteristic of the mature Shakespeare. The lines are closely packed with meaning, and we rarely find an image used purely for its emotional and descriptive content. Instead it is employed functionally for insult, for revealing a character, an attitude, or even a **theme**. Shakespeare seems to have disciplined his work very thoroughly, pruning away all excess. The austerity of the style is well suited to the subject of the play. **Rhyme** is very rare, and there are many run-on lines. In addition, there is a considerable amount of prose, particularly when Menenius, the tribunes, or the common people are involved.

A few major images dominate the play. These are mainly concerned with the body and its functions, and in particular, its ills. We must, of course, remember that Shakespeare took the image of the belly and the members straight out of Plutarch, but it was also an Elizabethan poetical and political commonplace to refer to the state in the same manner, in terms of the human body. There is also a great deal of reference to disease, and to the sometimes drastic therapeutic action needed to halt the spread of a contagious or infectious condition. At the same time we have many references to animals, usually ones whose attributes are not respected, such as the ass, dog, cur, goose, cat, crow, goat, mule, minnow, and camel. Such references are frequently found in the mouth of Coriolanus and used as insults.

THEMES

There are really two themes, political and personal, which are interwoven, and we should note that Shakespeare calls the play *The Tragedy of Coriolanus*, a title which shows the importance of the personal tragedy. But at the same time there is tremendous emphasis on the political **theme**, the ethics and nature of government, particularly in the Roman state, but with some oblique reference to the Jacobean situation.

The political **theme** is really based on a question: what is the best form of government? The play strives to give some kind of answer to this question though, as James E. Phillips points out, the critics cannot quite make up their minds as to what this answer may be. Shakespeare is showing sympathy with the oppressed, says one group; he is showing the evils of government by the people, says another; he is superbly impartial, says the third. What is really shown, says Professor Phillips, is the orthodox Elizabethan and Jacobean belief that everything has its ordered place in the commonwealth, and that all persons have both rights and duties. It is the failure of both Coriolanus and the people of Rome to exercise their rights sanely, and to fulfill their duties correctly, which brings about confusion in the state. Generally speaking, Shakespeare shows the evils of democracy, used in the classical sense to mean "government by the unbridled mob." He has sympathy with individual common folk, but he has little time for the many-headed monster, the rabble, which can be ruled all too easily by power-blinded demagogues. Rule by the aristocrats of Rome would seem to be the preferred alternative, but the aristocrats do not always fulfill their duties to the common people. Above all, the play seems to imply the necessity of some central organized authority.

Coriolanus, however, does not embody that authority because of his excessive pride, and here the political **theme** shades into the personal. While he knows his rights and pursues a consistent concept of personal duty, Coriolanus does not recognize the existence of larger aspects of public duty before which private duty must give way. The personal **theme** of the play concerns the growth of self-knowledge in Coriolanus, and, ironically, his recognition leads him to his destruction.

The play offers no easy answers to any of the questions it poses, and Shakespeare takes pains to show us the faults and the virtues of both the citizens and Coriolanus. In addition, he shows us the power plays of demagogues and conniving politicians who care for their own personal ends rather than the public good. In this respect, the evils of an absolutism based on appeals to the sometimes irrational instincts of the populace are also demonstrated. The modernity of vision shown here is quite remarkable.

THE PLOT

The play is very tightly constructed, plot and counterplot working against each other with great dramatic skill. Most of the action takes place in the public places and streets of Rome, as befits Shakespeare's most avowedly political play. The action begins with an uproar in a Roman street and the arrival of mutinous citizens armed with various weapons to growl against the patricians, the aristocrats of Rome, who, they say, have no care at all for the welfare of the starving common folk. The worst of all in this regard is the man they call Caius Marcius (later to receive the title of *Coriolanus*). He is opposed to giving the starving populace grain from the public stores at their own price, the price the people want to pay. Later we discover that they want the grain gratis, but Marcius believes that such a policy causes a weakening of the people's moral fiber. The citizens speak of the villainous pride of Caius Marcius and seem to hate him more than any other patrician. A representative of this hated class, Menenius Agrippa, then appears, and he speedily pacifies the mob by his rather illogical tale of the belly and the members, an anecdote aimed to show the mob the place and function of all groups of citizens in the general government of the state. He continually insists that the patricians have the greatest concern for the plebeians' welfare.

Just as things seem to have quieted down, Caius Marcius appears with news of another rabble which had appeared at the Senate chamber asking for food, and which had been pacified by receiving, not food, but political representation. The plebeians now have five tribunes to represent them, though we never meet more than two in the play, Sicinius Veleutus and Junius Brutus. Certainly Caius Marcius lives up to the reputation given him by the mob because he insults them in a singularly bitter manner and resents their growing political power.

News is then brought that the Volscians, a neighboring tribe, have raised an army against Rome, and the senators and tribunes are naturally levying a force to fight them. Marcius immediately says that he will fight because he wants to do battle with the Volscian leader, Tullus Aufidius, a valiant warrior. In the next scene we meet Aufidius and discover that he has an equal respect for the military valor of Coriolanus.

In the same act we are introduced to the principal feminine characters, particularly the strongwilled and almost masculine Volumnia, the mother of Caius Marcius, who had brought him up alone, since his father had died while the boy was a mere baby. Virgilia, the wife of Marcius, is also introduced, but she is soft-spoken and almost silent, a marked contrast to Volumnia, though she too has a strong will. Then there is the chaste maiden Valeria, a merry soul, and finally we hear about Young Marcius, Caius Marcius' son. The women all await news from the battlefield.

The next scene takes us to the battle, where Caius Marcius shouts insults at the troops who are too chickenhearted to follow him into danger. He finally rushes the gates of Corioli and is shut inside, alone. Nevertheless, he manages to fight so valiantly and do such damage that the city surrenders. Then he goes in search of more killing, meets Aufidius with some companions in battle and vanquishes the whole lot. Afterwards, the young man is offered a large share of the booty; but he hates to hear himself praised and turns down everything except a good warhorse and the title Coriolanus in token of his victory. The first act ends with Aufidius expressing hatred of the victor, Caius Marcius.

The second act shows various aspects of rejoicing in Rome, among the ladies and the patricians. Then when Coriolanus enters the city the people give him a tumultuous welcome as a returning hero. The senators are so impressed with Coriolanus as a soldier that they decide to appoint him Consul. However, it is the custom that any candidate for that office must stand in the market place and show his wounds and scars to the people and ask for their votes. Coriolanus does not want to do this, partly because he hates to hear his noble deeds praised, since he thinks them mere duty, and partly because he is too proud to humble himself before the common people.

Under protest, Coriolanus goes down to the market place and asks the people for their voices. However, he avoids showing his wounds, and his manner in asking for votes is by no means humble. As a result the people give their voices, but feel rather doubtful about what they have done. The tribunes, Sicinius and Brutus, then appear, and in furtherance of their plan to prevent Coriolanus' election they persuade the people to revoke their consent. The tribunes do not seem to be acting from patriotic motives here, but rather they seem afraid that Coriolanus might take away power from their office.

In the third act the tribunes' plan goes into effect and the people revoke their decision. Coriolanus is most enraged about the situation, and Sicinius and Brutus lead him on. Then a mob of citizens appears and is inflamed by the oratory of the tribunes into calling for Coriolanus to be executed as a traitor. Caius Marcius and his group are forced to flee. All his friends then try to persuade Coriolanus that he ought to be humble and apologize to the plebeians, but he steadfastly refuses until his mother, Volumnia, finally shames him into appearing to humble himself. But again Coriolanus loses his temper and insults the mob which now calls for banishment, on pain of a traitor's death should he ever return to Rome. In a rage Coriolanus curses the multitude and says that he refuses to be banished by them; instead he will banish Rome. He must have the initiative.

The fourth act shows the departure of Coriolanus from Rome. He tries to cheer everyone else up, particularly the women in his family. Then he goes to Antium to the house of Aufidius where he offers to fight by the side of his former enemy against Rome, his native city. Coriolanus is now seeking personal revenge on the entire population of Rome since no one, not even members of his own patrician class, intervened against the mob. Aufidius greets Caius Marcius Coriolanus with open arms and gives him joint command of the Volscian army. He honestly admires the military prowess of the Roman and is proud to march under the same banner with him. Here we see the best and most generous side of Aufidius.

In the meantime things are very quiet in Rome, and apparently everything is calm while the two tribunes talk with self-satisfaction of their part in the banishment of Coriolanus. They tell Menenius that Rome is much better off without his protégé, and the old patrician says that no one, not even his family, knows where Coriolanus is.

We are then returned to Antium, where we find that Aufidius is beginning to feel some jealousy of the valor of Coriolanus. The best soldiers of Aufidius flock to his rival, whose every word seems to show his old arrogance. It is impossible for Coriolanus to remain long in a subordinate position, and at times it is difficult to tell who is the senior man, Aufidius or Coriolanus. Nevertheless, the Volscian is a politic man and, as we see in the last act, he is prepared to wait until Rome has been captured to find some way to attack Coriolanus, accuse him of treason, and regain his old ascendancy among his own people.

Meanwhile the news of Coriolanus' alliance with the Volscians has struck terror to the Romans, who now desire to be reconciled to the man they had so willingly banished. The mob even turns against the tribunes, whose very lives are in danger. Rome also sends emissaries to Coriolanus in the hope that he will relent and spare the city. At the beginning of the fifth act the mission looks quite impossible: Coriolanus refuses to speak to his old general, Cominius, and sends Menenius away with a broken heart.

Then the three ladies in Coriolanus' life come to see him: Virgilia, his wife, Volumnia, his mother, and Valeria, their friend, together with Young Marcius, his son. Virgilia says very little, but from her demeanor and Coriolanus' reaction we can see that he is deeply touched. Then Volumnia pleads with her son, and insists on speaking despite all his protestations against her. She tries emotional arguments, political arguments, and finally, through her apparent contempt, she brings him to understand that the noblest action is for him to follow the road of mercy and spare Rome. This he decides to do, though he seems quite sure that this action will be the cause of his death. He sends the ladies home to Rome where they are welcomed as befits heroines. He himself stays among the Volscians in order to justify his conduct and show that he acted properly.

The action of sparing Rome has now given Aufidius his opportunity and he begins to plot against Coriolanus to bring about his death, yet in such a way that his own action is considered justified. In a letter to the Volscian lords Aufidius accuses Coriolanus of treachery, and they are ready to listen to his arguments when the Roman warrior enters Antium in triumph, despite his failure to take Rome. Aufidius openly calls Caius Marcius a traitor and then insults him by saying that he sold the chance to take Rome for a few tears from his mother's eyes. Coriolanus cannot bear to be taunted so he offers violence to the entire Volscian company. The people, fickle as they are, now shout for his blood. In the confusion Coriolanus is struck down by the weapon of a conspirator and Aufidius stands on his corpse. Note that this death is not at all honorable; it is really a kind of conspiratorial execution.

The moment Coriolanus is dead the Volscians repent of their haste and remember his nobility. A lord tells Aufidius not to stand on such a great man, and he obeys. Instead of justifying his behavior he speaks a sincere and noble assessment of such a brave and honest man. Arrangements are then made for a splendid funeral, and the body of Caius Marcius Coriolanus, the man of so much potential and so little actual achievement, is borne off with military honors.

CORIOLANUS

TEXTUAL ANALYSIS

ACT I

ACT I: SCENE I

Though this play is entitled *The Tragedy of Coriolanus*, the hero does not appear immediately. The first scene is laid in a street of Rome, where a great deal of the action takes place. A company of mutinous citizens, armed with staves, clubs, and other weapons, enters. The First Citizen comes in inciting the people to riot, asking them if they are prepared to die rather than starve. Needless to say, the crowd affirm this resolution. The First Citizen then claims that Caius Marcius is the "chief enemy to the people." The crowd all agree with him and the First Citizen suggests that they should kill Caius Marcius so that they can get corn at their own price, which is not specified.

Comment: This scene takes us immediately into the heart of the trouble and rebellion in Rome. Shakespeare, as usual, employs his opening scene for the purpose of exposition, of bringing his

audience to grips with the central situation of the play. Here too he introduces us to the citizenry of Rome who will be, collectively speaking, one of the most important characters in the play. At the same time he introduces us to Caius Marcius.

Another thing we should note here is that customarily in England the word "corn" means not Indian Corn, but what Americans term wheat or grain. The people of Rome are therefore starving because they have insufficient grain to make bread.

The First Citizen then proceeds to give a list of grievances against the patricians, the aristocratic class of ancient Rome. He claims that the citizens are despised while the patricians are by contrast considered good. In his anger he accuses the aristocrats of having plenty to eat, while the common people starve, and he wishes that the ruling class would at least let the people have the stored crop surplus before it goes bad. The First Citizen is really quite a demagogue too, because he incites his listeners by telling them that the suffering of the common people is actually useful to the aristocrats, who wish to keep things that way because the people, being weak from hunger, will thus be easier to control. The First Citizen suggests, however, that the common people "revenge this with our pikes ere we become rakes." His motive, he says, is to gain food, not just revenge.

Comment: Shakespeare has changed his source, Plutarch's *Life of Caius Marcius Coriolanus*, by putting the corn riots at this point of the action. It does, of course, give a dramatic opening, and also introduces the basic conflict of the play, the common citizens against the aristocrats of ancient Rome. In addition, the reduction of two separate insurrections to one

further compresses the action for the maximum effect. Some critics think that Shakespeare in dramatizing this particular situation is making a topical reference to a contemporary event, an insurrection in the Midland Counties of England in 1607, which had the same cause. The people were hungry and wanted cheap supplies of corn. (See Pettet in Bibliography.) This is part of the evidence which dates the play around 1608.

Note too that the Citizens speak prose rather than poetry, though they indulge in the packed and elliptical (shortened) sentences found in Shakespeare's mature style.

Finally the Second Citizen manages to get a hearing; he has been trying for some time to get the attention of the crowd. Now he asks the First Citizen whether he plans to turn particularly against Caius Marcius, to which question the First Citizen retorts indignantly that Caius Marcius acts like a dog to the common people.

Comment: In Shakespeare's plays the dog is often shown as an animal with unpleasant characteristics. Caius Marcius is thus being introduced with his worst attributes shown first. The use of animal epithets is frequent in this play, particularly in insulting speeches, and the reader should pay close attention to them.

The Second Citizen, who seems more moderate than the First Citizen, then recalls Caius Marcius' services to his country, and suggests that these should not be forgotten. The First Citizen says that he knows them very well indeed and would take them into consideration, but for the fact that Caius Marcius repays himself for this valor by being proud. Despite the rebuke of the other speaker that such a remark smacks of malice, the First Citizen continues his attack by claiming that, whatever men may say to the contrary, Caius Marcius has acted valiantly in order to gain personal glory. In addition, the desire for glory, the Roman virtus, or "valiantness," was not so much for the service of his country, but in order to please his mother and also to gratify his own over-powering pride. The Second Citizen tries to calm his compatriot by saying that one cannot blame a man for acting according to his nature. After all, Caius Marcius is not a vicious man, and certainly one thing is in his favor: no one can accuse him of personal greed. But the First Citizen is too angry to listen and says that Caius Marcius is absolutely full of faults. The debate is then interrupted by a new noise of rioting. Apparently the other half of the city has risen in rebellion against the patricians.

Comment: This part of the scene is important for its function in introducing Caius Marcius to us. It gives us a sketch of both his faults and his virtues, with, of course, the emphasis on the faults. Shakespeare is using here the same technique as that of Antony and Cleopatra where he had a couple of Roman soldiers show the vices and weaknesses of Mark Antony. Incidentally, the use of citizens for the purposes of this debate is important because Shakespeare frequently employs unnamed common people, servants, etc., to give honest and unsophisticated comments on major characters. Here, for instance, we see mixed reactions to Caius Marcius. The scene also prepares for the introduction of Volumnia, Marcius' mother, who will become important later on.

Most important, however, the scene raises the question of the hero's motives in seeking virtus. Now this "valiantness" was one of the most prized of the Roman virtues, and our own word is but a corruption of it. It meant unselfish service and unswerving loyalty to the cause of military honor, and also civil honor under the aegis of the Roman state. Of course, along with this attitude went an unspoken, but necessary, pursuit of the ideal of personal honor-but always the state was supposed to come first.

At this rather chaotic moment Menenius Agrippa enters. He is an elderly man, a patrician, but "one that hath always loved the people," and even the First Citizen admits that "He's one honest enough." Immediately Menenius addresses himself to the crowd, calling them "my countrymen," and asking why they are armed with staffs and clubs. The First Citizen is not long in replying, and very insolently too. He says that the Roman senate knows very well what the matter is, and what is more, it has known for the past two weeks. The people are now out of patience so they're about to make the patricians listen by force of arms. The poor petitioners have strong arms as well as strong breaths.

Comment: This continual mentioning of the evil smell belonging to the breath of the common people has often been taken as evidence of Shakespeare's own personal attitude, and his undemocratic point of view. Such an opinion does not seem warranted by the evidence; after all, this could be just a common allegation, and perhaps a statement of fact. Further, it is an error to claim that Shakespeare himself held all the opinions he put into the mouths of his characters.

Menenius, however, seems unlike the typical patrician as drawn by the First Citizen. He tries to ingratiate himself with the citizenry of Rome by addressing them as "masters, my good friends, mine honest neighbors." Then he questions the wisdom of their decision to rebel against the patricians. He tries reason and tells the mutinous citizens that the patricians take most loving care of them, and far from blaming the patricians for the scarcity they should recognize that they are wrong in raising a rebellion against the Roman state. It, like heaven itself, will simply proceed on its appointed course whatever happens. Anyway, the gods are responsible for the dearth, not the patricians. The citizens would therefore be better advised to kneel and offer sacrifice to the gods rather than to raise a rebellion against their political rulers.

Menenius also takes care to give the citizens a way out by claiming that he can of course see that they are almost out of their minds with the calamity that has befallen them. Naturally that is the reason they are making such totally false allegations against the heads of the state who care for the common people the way fathers care for their children. This last comment provokes a derisive snort from the First Citizen, who launches into a recital of the real and imagined woes of the populace. Again he claims that the patricians don't care about the starving people of Rome. They are letting the common people die while they themselves have grain stored away for their own use. They repeal acts which are against the interests of the rich, while at the same time passing others to make life harder for the poor. Menenius listens patiently to this outburst and then starts to tell a very homely tale in order to pacify the rebellious crowd.

Comment: The attitude of Menenius towards the citizens is in some respects less flattering to them than they realize. Menenius may greet them civilly,

but he remains an aristocrat through and through, and he has given away his own opinions on the nature of government by saying that the patricians care for the people as fathers care for their children. This indicates a specific philosophy of rule, and it is really the initial policy of Rome in this play. Rome is an aristocracy, a government of the rich people, the nobles, the property holders, the ones who have the greatest economic interest in the country. Such a definition was also orthodox Elizabethan and Jacobean political theory and it could be found in such works as Aristotle's Politics. Good aristocrats would thus consider the commonalty as children, who by implication would not know what was best for them. Consequently, they would need constant care on the part of the patricians, whose very name derives from the Latin word for father, pater.

Menenius then begins his most famous speech, the anecdote on the revolt of limbs against the belly. As the elderly statesman tells the story the people listen to the way in which the members began openly to complain of the uselessness of the belly sitting in the middle of the body merely absorbing all the food put into it, and unlike the limbs and senses, playing no active part and doing no work. All the other bodily functions seem to contribute to the general welfare of the body, except the lazy belly. By now Menenius is having a very good time with his captive audience and starts to act out his part with artistic embellishments. He will make the belly smile as well as speak, for instance. In this approach he shows not only a good sense of humor, but also a firm grasp of the principles of telling a good story. Having claimed that the belly will speak, he resorts to a rhetorical device and digresses, or turns aside, from his apparent desire to entertain and goes on to his main purpose, comparing the fictional situation with the attitude of the citizens towards the senators of Rome.

By this time the impatient First Citizen interrupts and tells Menenius to hurry up, but he has fallen into a trap set rather adroitly by Menenius, because he immediately starts praising the limbs and the other functions of the body at the expense of the belly. The patrician cuts in with a joking "tut, tut," because the First Citizen seems to be taking the floor away from him. Nevertheless, the citizen continues with his thesis, calling the belly a cormorant, as though it were the greedy bird that would eat anything.

The old storyteller, Menenius, still bides his time and then, when he has everyone's attention, he continues with his tale. He, of course, takes the side of the belly, and demolishes the argument of the First Citizen. Certainly the belly agrees that he receives all the food, and so he should as the storehouse and shop of the body. But then, he continues, his task is to send all this nourishment throughout the various nooks and crannies of the body in order that every portion should receive its proper nourishment. In fact the entire body lives off the belly, which sends forth nothing except what is good and useful, while it is left with only the waste products.

Menenius now zeroes in on the citizens and applies this parable specifically to the current situation in Rome. The senators of Rome, he claims, are the belly, while the citizens are the "mutinous members." And like the belly, the Senate has nothing but the public welfare as its aim.

Comment: This particular anecdote is one of the most important statements on government in the play. It is found in essentially the same form in

Plutarch, but Shakespeare has added details from another source, Camden's Remaines. In addition, this image of the state as a human body was an Elizabethan and Jacobean commonplace so that writers frequently referred to "the body politic" as opposed to the physical body of man, the microcosm, the little world, and the universe, the macrocosm or the great world. The Roman state is therefore a body liable to disease and decay, and throughout the play we will find continual reference to the state in general in terms of the metaphor of the human body and its attendant illnesses.

At the same time we should note that Menenius is not reasoning logically in this argument, but the argument does well enough for the mutinous citizens who are not particularly skilled in the arts of rhetoric or disputation. Menenius deliberately argues in a circle, "begging the question" as one might put it in terms of logic. He assumes the truth of what he is trying to prove. Why does he choose the belly as the equivalent of the Senate when one would logically expect him to choose the head to indicate the reasonableness of the rulers of Rome? Obviously the answer is simply that he wishes to prove a point whose truth is already so obvious to him that it requires no proof. Therefore he picks only that evidence which supports his preconceived opinion.

He continues by asking the First Citizen what he thinks and then humorously insults him by calling him the "great toe" of the assembly, since he is "one o' th' lowest, basest, poorest/ Of this most wise rebellion." Here, of course, Menenius is using **irony**, saying the opposite of what he believes about the insurrection.

But then he rounds on the First Citizen and the crowd saying that Rome and her rats (obviously he means the mob) are at the point of civil war, in the course of which one or the other must be destroyed.

Just at this inopportune moment Caius Marcius enters, and he promptly lives up to the derogatory remarks that have been made about him. He insults the citizenry and in his opening image betrays his attitude towards them. They have made themselves scabby by "rubbing the poor itch" of their "opinion." Their minds and their policies are therefore diseased. The First Citizen comments ironically "We have ever your good word," and in reply Marcius begins a tirade against the crowd, calling them curs, hares, and geese rather than lions and foxes.

Comment: Note how Caius Marcius refers to the commons in terms of disease, or as dirty, frightened, stupid animals who are easily led. Always look carefully at the epithets Marcius applies to those who are inferior to him. They tell us a lot about him.

According to Marcius the mob of citizens is fickle, and no more to be depended on than "the coal of fire upon the ice."

Comment: This comparison seems at first a trifle obscure, but it is thought to be a topical reference to the unusually severe frost of January 1607-1608 when the river Thames froze over so thickly that it was possible to walk across it. Apparently a kind of winter carnival was held and fires were built upon the ice.

In other words, the favor of the people soon melts away, the way the fire melts the ice, or the way a hailstone melts in the sun. The commons are so lacking in virtue that they taint any man who trusts them so that anyone who thinks himself great is better advised to gain their hate than their love. They cannot be depended upon, and making use of them would be like trying to swim with fins of lead or trying to cut down an oak tree with rushes. In short, the people are a useless lot, quite capable of turning upon their former heroes and destroying them. Were it not for the careful government and control of the Senate the populace would probably destroy itself.

Comment: This remains Caius Marcius' opinion throughout the play, and the evidence of events seems to bear it out.

He then asks Menenius what on earth the people want and is told that they want corn at their own price.

Comment: What they really want is corn distributed free of charge, a policy which was generally considered to have brought about the downfall of Athens because it took away from the people their initiative and their desire to work.

Caius Marcius is enraged at the audacity of the populace in daring to question the nobles and their policies. He again expresses his contempt for the people and claims that their conduct weakens the general structure of the government. He wishes aloud that the nobles would cease to feel pity for the starving common folk and instead permit him to inflict physical punishment on them.

But Marcius has some strange news to bring to Menenius from the council chamber of the Roman Senate. The other group of the common people had presented a petition to the

Senate, playing upon the sympathy of the patricians and saying that the gods did not send corn only for the good of the rich. The patricians then granted the petition, but its strangeness still puzzles and angers Caius Marcius. Indeed, it does seem irrelevant to the alleged purpose of the riots - corn gratis. The people have been granted a kind of political representation, five tribunes to be chosen by them to present their wrongs to the nobles. Junius Brutus and Sicinius are two who have been chosen, and they are the only ones we meet in this play. Caius Marcius is disturbed by the precedent and looks ahead to a time when this policy will cause greater revolution than at present. He sees it as a weakening of the central authority and wishes that he had been allowed to crush this particular rebellion by military force.

Comment: Shakespeare seems to alter things a trifle here because, in *Plutarch*, Junius Brutus and Sicinius were "the causers and procurers of this sedition." Marcius' additional comment on the danger of recognizing the political ambitions of the rabble is important as one of the major political attitudes of this highly political play. There seems to be an overriding fear of what we today consider to be the most highly desirable form of government - democracy, government by people. But to the audience of Shakespeare's day democracy was highly undesirable because it would automatically mean the destruction of a centralized government based on a belief in the divinely appointed authority of the monarch. As a result, the people were expected to obey the monarch at all times and at all costs.

This concept, transferred to the insurrection in Rome, means that the people are automatically wrong

because they are rebelling against the authority of the patricians whom seventeenth-century political writers would consider as divinely appointed to do what was best for the people. Misfortunes such as the famine at the beginning of the play would therefore have been sent by God, or the gods, as punishment for the sins of the people who ought patiently to bear them in reparation for their guilt.

Shakespeare uses this concept of divinely constituted authority very frequently throughout his dramas, particularly in the history plays, and in *Troilus and Cressida* (I.iii) he has the character of Ulysses speak of the chaos that results when the accepted rigid system of order and degree is violated. Small wonder, then, that Caius Marcius should fear the participation of the people in the government. Such a policy would pervert its original ends and would leave the state open to the fickle demands of the unbridled desires of the mob-or so the patricians would think. The centralized government represented by a monarchy, or by an aristocracy, was distinctly preferable in the orthodox opinion of Shakespeare's day.

Almost with disgust Caius Marcius orders the populace to go home, and at that moment the two new tribunes Sicinius and Brutus enter along with some unnamed senators and two generals, Cominius and Titus Lartius. This group brings the news to Marcius that the Volsces, enemies of Rome, have taken up arms against the city. Immediately Marcius is all warrior and he rejoices in the possibility of war. After all, as he says, the Volscians have a leader named Tullus Aufidius who is a thoroughly noble man and a good soldier. In fact he is the only person with whom Marcius himself would change places.

Cominius, the general, asks if the two have fought each other, and Caius Marcius generously replies "He is a lion/ That I am proud to hunt." So great a warrior is this Aufidius that he would wish to make war only with him, and would even change sides to fight against him should they chance to be on the same side.

Comment: Note this characterization of Aufidius by his bitterest enemy, because later on in the play he seems less noble than Marcius makes him in this introduction. It is, however, important that Tullus Aufidius be made such a noble person at the beginning of the play; otherwise the prowess of Caius Marcius would be lessened. There is also an ironic parallel between this tribute and the epitaph, the elegy over the dead Coriolanus, which is spoken by Aufidius at the close of the play. In addition we see further irony through our knowledge that Caius Marcius will indeed change sides to fight as an ally of Tullus Aufidius, not his enemy.

The senators then tell Marcius to go with Cominius to this war against the Volscians. Titus Lartius, though an old man, promptly declares his intention of throwing away his stick and going along as well. The senators then order the people home and Sicinius and Brutus are left alone on the stage discussing the events. Within a moment they start pulling the character of Caius Marcius to pieces. Sicinius sees him as a totally proud man, and Brutus agrees, adding the hope that the war will rid Rome of him. The man has become so proud through his valor that he cannot be borne. Sicinius then wonders aloud how such a proud man can bear to work under the command of Cominius. Brutus in reply gives an explanation which in some respects tells us more about the tribune himself than about Marcius.

He claims that Caius Marcius actually prefers the subordinate position in order to preserve his own personal reputation for complete success. Consequently the general will be blamed whenever anything goes wrong, and public opinion will praise Marcius more and wish that he had been in command.

> **Comment: Here Brutus sees Caius Marcius in his own likeness. This kind of calculated political trickery is quite foreign to the patrician warrior, but natural to the conniving professional politician. Here we begin to understand the smallness of Brutus' mind. Caius Marcius has different motives; personal honor and the pursuit of an ideal of individual virtus, or valor.**

Sicinius agrees with the incorrect assessment, and Brutus goes on to say that Cominius in fact deserves half the honor that the general reputation gives to Caius Marcius, who does not really merit the high opinion in which he is held.

Summary: This first scene is an admirable introduction to the action of the play and also to the chief **themes** and characters.

1. It introduces us to the major conflict of the play, that between the rebellious citizens and the patricians.

2. It gives us the opinion of the citizenry concerning Caius Marcius, an opinion which is unabashedly hostile.

3. Caius Marcius is introduced in the worst possible light as a man who lacks diplomacy and who dislikes the common people.

4. We meet Menenius, the patrician, the voice of moderation, who manages to get along quite well with

the citizens, chiefly because of his sense of humor and homely language.

5. It introduces the chief opposition to Caius Marcius in the persons of the tribunes Sicinius and Brutus.

6. It hints at the chief political thesis of the play, that rule by an aristocracy, an elite ruling class with absolute authority, is preferable to a government in which representatives of the people are included.

7. It prepares for the introduction of Volumnia, the mother of Caius Marcius.

8. It introduces the military **theme** of the play through the coming war with the Volscians and points towards the revelation of the other side of Caius Marcius' character - that of the warrior.

9. Aufidius, the military foil to Caius Marcius, is introduced, and he is shown as a noble warrior. Even Marcius, who is not generally given to praising anyone, thinks highly of him.

ACT I: SCENE II

The scene now shifts to the senate chamber of the Volscian town of Corioles (sometimes called Corioli), where a discussion is taking place among Tullus Aufidius and the assembled senators. Obviously both the Romans and Volscians have their spies, because Aufidius notes that the Romans always seem to have advance knowledge of the Volscian plans. He himself has also received a letter from Rome telling of the famine riots and giving news of the Roman mobilization, probably against Corioles. The letter even names the generals, Cominius, Titus Lartius, and of course Marcius, who is listed to Aufidius as "your old enemy." The Volscian general regrets that the premature discovery of the plans means that the army can no longer proceed with its original intention to capture many smaller towns before Rome awakened to its danger. Then, in a situation parallel to that of the preceding scene, Aufidius looks forward to a meeting with Caius Marcius, saying that they have sworn to fight to the death at their next meeting. The senators wish Aufidius well and all withdraw.

Comment And Summary: This short scene serves to introduce Aufidius in his own person and also to reveal the plans of both Volscians and Romans. It establishes the mutual respect that Aufidius and Caius Marcius have for each other and therefore points toward their future meeting.

ACT 1: SCENE III

This scene takes place in the house of Caius Marcius, and it is totally different in tone from the preceding hurly-burly of the play. Volumnia and Virgilia, the mother and wife of Caius Marcius, enter, and setting down two low stools, they start sewing. This action immediately indicates the domestic nature of the scene. Volumnia commences by trying to cheer up the preoccupied Virgilia, begging her to sing, or at least to sound more cheerful. She claims that if she were married to Caius Marcius she would rejoice more in an absence by which he gains honor than in his loving presence in bed. Then, in what may be an attempt to shame her daughter-in-law, Volumnia recalls how she sent her son to the wars when he was but a young boy. To her delight he returned with a garland of oak leaves on his head in token of having saved the life of a Roman citizen in battle. She claims that she was just as elated at this sight as she had been when she had learned that she had borne a boy child.

Virgilia, however, asks Volumnia what her reaction would have been had Marcius been killed. To this question Volumnia proudly replies that then the honor he had gained in the engagement would have been sufficient to take the place of her son. She says that if she had had a dozen sons she would prefer that eleven should die nobly for their country rather than that one should avoid battle because of softness and overindulgence.

Comment: This exchange is most important because it reveals the characters of the two women. Volumnia shows herself a severe, upright, honor-seeking Roman matron for whom personal integrity and valor are to be pursued to the exclusion of all other considerations of love. Virgilia, on the other hand, in a one-line speech reveals herself as a loving and tender wife with little liking for the dangers of war. Where the mother thinks of honor and personal valor, the wife thinks of personal danger.

Note

In some sources of the story of Caius Marcius the name of the wife is given as Volumnia and that of the mother as Veturia. Shakespeare follows Plutarch for his assignment of names.

This contrast is enhanced by the way in which the timid and shrinking Virgilia wishes to retire when the lady Valeria is announced. Volumnia, of course, will not permit her to do so, and proceeds with a speech which recreates in her imagination what is probably going on in Corioli, with Caius Marcius defeating Aufidius and urging his troops on to action though he himself is covered with blood. The mention of blood is too much for Virgilia, who shudders with fear, "O Jupiter, no blood!" This comment seems to Volumnia to be a confession of weakness and she scornfully tells Virgilia that blood becomes a warrior better than the gilt on his monument. Then she goes on to declare that the forehead of Hector when it spouted forth in blood from a Grecian sword looked lovelier than the breasts of Hecuba when she suckled her son. Virgilia is almost overcome by the savagery of Volumnia's denial of the primacy of a mother's love and utters a prayer that Caius Marcius may be protected from Aufidius. The dauntless Volumnia only replies contemptuously that Marcius will utterly defeat his enemy.

A third contrast is then supplied with the arrival of the lady Valeria. She is a merry person who seems to have come visiting with the avowed purpose of cheering up the ladies whose man is away at the war. Incidentally, she represents a third kind of Roman lady, a noble and virtuous maiden, as opposed to Volumnia the stern matron, and Virgilia the gentle, loving wife.

As soon as she enters, Valeria, with consummate tact, asks Virgilia after the health of her son. Virgilia merely replies in a few words, but Volumnia takes over the conversation and insists on the warlike proclivities of her grandson. Valeria laughs merrily and tells of the way she saw the child run after a butterfly which he caught and accidentally let go. In its pursuit he fell down and when he caught it he tore it to pieces with his teeth. The reactions to this cruel act, reminiscent of the tales of the Emperor Nero, are indeed interesting. Volumnia is immediately reminded of one of Caius Marcius' moods, something that informs us about both Volumnia and her son. Valeria thinks the incident indicates nobility and seems amused, but Virgilia says that he is "a crack" (an imp) to act so. She is disapproving.

Valeria, however, has not come merely to be sociable. She invites the ladies to go with her to visit a woman who has recently given birth. Virgilia says that she cannot go, and indicates that she is waiting for news of her husband, which Valeria promptly mentions now that she is reminded. She tells how Marcius and Titus Lartius are encamped outside the walls of Corioli waiting for something to happen. Once again Valeria begs Virgilia to go with her to Volumnia, but finally the wife's gentle stubbornness wins the day, and she stays home.

SUMMARY

This scene reveals the characters of the women in the life of Caius Marcius.

1. Volumnia, his mother, is a stern, warlike Roman matron, not much given to sympathy, and impatient of anything that smacks of feminine weakness. She claims to glory in the warlike skill of her only son and she despises cowardice. The relationship between Marcius and his mother is hinted at here.

2. Virgilia, the wife, is later addressed by Caius Marcius as "My gracious silence," and indeed that is a good description of her. She is sensitive, outwardly weak, yet at the same time possessed of a quiet obstinacy that gets her own way when she is convinced that she is right.

3. In Valeria we have a foil character to the other two women, and also a fine example of a Roman maiden: virtuous, merry, yet at the same time subscribing to the Roman attitudes toward war.

4. Through the description of Young Marcius' treatment of the harmless butterfly we get a glimpse of the blind cruelty of his father, something that Volumnia would apparently praise.

ACT I: SCENES IV-V

The scene takes place outside the walls of Corioli. Marcius and Titus Lartius, the old general, are trying to discover whether Cominius has yet begun an engagement with the Volsces. The Romans then sound a parley, but the people of Corioli say that their armies are about to sally forth to fight the Romans for whom they have no fear. Like Aufidius himself, not a single man is intimidated by the reputation of Caius Marcius.

Marcius then exhorts his own troops to fight bravely, but it is no use and the Romans are beaten back to their trenches. Then, at the moment of what seems like defeat, Caius Marcius turns on his troops with a flood of invective like that of a non-commissioned officer cursing his troops back into the battle. He wishes plagues and diseases upon his cowardly soldiers, calls them geese with the souls of geese, and then threatens to destroy them himself. He calls on them to follow him through the gates of Corioli, but no one does, and the gates close, leaving Marcius alone inside the enemy city. The troops naturally consider that he is finished, and tell Titus Lartius accordingly. The old general speaks of the valor of Marcius as though he were already dead, but suddenly the man himself appears, bleeding profusely, but still fighting. Heartened by the sight, the entire army enters the city.

Roman soldiers now appear, but they are discussing booty, not the glory of war, when Marcius and Titus Lartius appear.

Marcius expresses his disgust with this attitude when he suddenly catches sight of Aufidius. Leaving Titus Lartius to make sure of the city, he sets off to help Cominius, followed by those soldiers who still have spirit left. Titus tries to dissuade him by saying that he is in no condition to continue fighting, but Marcius refuses to withdraw. The blood he has shed is "physical" (healthful) for him rather than anything else. He says he is hardly even warmed to the fight and so he sets out to find Aufidius. Titus remains behind and calls for a trumpet sound in the market place to summon the town officials of Corioli to speak with him.

Comment And Summary

In these two scenes we see Caius Marcius as a soldier. He is brave, and indeed rather foolhardy, but certainly extremely skillful in battle to have been able to survive as a lone Roman fighting within the walls of an enemy city. The Roman soldiers on the whole don't seem to measure up to the standard of bravery set by Marcius and he castigates them in language which makes them sound quite loathsome. He possesses tremendous endurance and singleness of purpose in his pursuit of Aufidius. Fighting makes a superman out of him.

ACT I: SCENE VI

The scene now shifts to another part of the battlefield where Cominius has been hotly engaged with the enemy. He has temporarily retired to regroup his forces and he speaks words of courage to his soldiers, telling them that their comrades are supporting them elsewhere. This speech is interrupted by the arrival of a messenger who says that he has had a very difficult time avoiding Volscian pursuers. He gives the impression that things are in a very bad way, that Caius Marcius and Titus Lartius have been driven to their trenches. But before Cominius can fully digest this bad news, a bloody apparition comes into view and is recognized as Caius Marcius.

The opening words of Marcius are typical, "Am I too late?" Such a speech from a man literally covered with blood indicates unusual courage. Cominius greets him with relief, but is disturbed about his wounds. The two soldiers then embrace and Marcius' speech bears careful examination:

O, let me clip ye
In arms as sound as when I wooed, in heart
As merry as when our nuptial day was done,
And tapers burned to bedward! (I.vi.29-32)

Comment: This comparison is important in a double sense. First it signifies in part the relationship between Marcius and Virgilia, if the happiest day of his life was his wedding day. Secondly, however, it indicates that Marcius is equally married to war, and that both war and his wife seem to rank together in his mind and heart.

Marcius tells how Titus Lartius is busy meting out justice in Corioli, but Cominius enquires about the apparently false information brought by the messenger. Caius Marcius then tells of the course of the battle and starts to insult his troops again, saying that they don't deserve political representation, because they have shown themselves so cowardly in action.

Comment: This brief exchange reinforces the idea of Marcius' total devotion to war, and it also contrasts him with Cominius who, even when he is forced to retire, doesn't insult his troops. Note too the way that Caius Marcius brings up his own greatest grievance against the common people: they have obtained political representation, but they are unworthy of it.

Marcius, never one to waste time in battle, then asks where the enemy's most trustworthy troops are located, and hearing that the Antiates under Aufidius are in the vanguard, he asks to be set opposite them. Cominius suggests that perhaps Marcius needs a bath and medical treatment, but the young man hotheadedly refuses. He calls for troops to follow him and rouses the men to a frenzy of patriotism by asking which of them are worth four of the enemy and equal to Aufidius in valor. The troops shout and cheer him, and Marcius picks four companions.

Comment: The last part of this scene shows Marcius in his real element - destruction. He is a valiant soldier and as a result can manage to command the loyalty of the troops. There is, however, a certain irony which looks ahead into the next act which shows Marcius in a political situation. Here he manages to gain the support of Cominius' troops by means of unaffectedly displaying his wounds and the blood he has shed for Rome.

SUMMARY

This scene shows more aspects of Marcius as a soldier.

1. He is hotheaded, impatient, and will not leave the battle though he is wounded. He even goes looking for further engagements, despite his earlier performance in Corioli.

2. His attitude towards the normal, timorous common soldier is just the same as his attitude towards the common people in Rome.

3. He remembers the political aspirations of the citizens, and of their military counterparts, even in the midst of battle. Obviously their success in politics rankles.

4. His contemptuous attitude towards the soldiers is contrasted with the more friendly one of the older man, Cominius.

5. He shows himself just as strongly and as joyfully wedded to war as to his wife, Virgilia.

6. The character of Aufidius is again mentioned as being noble, and Marcius considers him a worthy opponent.

7. Despite his brusqueness Marcius can command the respect of his men because of his valor. His warlike aspect shows his best side, on the whole.

ACT I: SCENES VII-VIII

The first scene takes place inside Corioli where Titus Lartius sets a guard on the city and goes to join Cominius and Caius Marcius.

The next scene begins with the entry of Marcius and Aufidius from different doors. The two valiant soldiers insult each other verbally at first, a common **convention** of **epic** single combat. Next, each boasts of his own military prowess, and then they fight. Some Volscians come to Aufidius' aid, but Marcius fights with all of them and finally drives them away. Disconsolate, Aufidius retires.

Comment And Summary: These scenes really serve as a link between the earlier, successful battle, and the praise of Marcius which is forthcoming. Also, scene viii arranges for the confrontation between Marcius and Aufidius. Here, of course, Marcius is successful, and the fact that he vanquishes not only Aufidius, but also his "certain Volscians" shows his superiority to his enemy.

ACT I: SCENE IX

This scene is laid in the Roman camp and opens with a flourish of trumpets, and the sounding of a retreat. Cominius enters, and then Marcius, from another door, with his wounded arm bound up in a scarf. Cominius joyfully congratulates Marcius on his success and claims that Rome will thank the gods she has such a brave soldier once he, as Marcius' superior officer, reports the brave deeds of the young man. Titus Lartius then enters with his troops and Cominius begins to tell him of the valorous behavior of Caius Marcius. Almost rudely Marcius interrupts to say that he can't bear praise, even from his mother. He has done his duty towards his country, and any man who has done that has acted in a more praiseworthy manner than he. Cominius refuses to allow such modesty, but Marcius demurs, saying that his wounds hurt him when anyone speaks either of them or of his valor. Nevertheless Cominius persists and assigns Caius Marcius a tenth of the total treasure taken in the capture of Corioli. The young warrior refuses this offer, saying that it would merely be a bribe to pay for his sword; he will simply accept what would normally be due to him. At this the trumpets blare; the army shouts his name; the soldiers throw their caps in the air; and Titus Lartius and Cominius stand bareheaded in tribute.

Marcius almost rudely brushes aside all this pomp and circumstance, saying that all this praise of him is mere exaggeration, even hypocrisy. Cominius repeats that he is too modest and then crowns him with a garland of victory, announcing at the same time that he gives Marcius as a free gift his own war horse, complete with harness. In addition, because of the deeds done at Corioli, he suggests that in the future the young man be known as Caius Marcius Coriolanus. There is another flourish of trumpets; the army shouts; and Caius Marcius says "I will go wash." He affirms that he is blushing with embarrassment, but says he will accept the horse, and of course, the title.

Comment: Marcius is not merely modest; instead he deplores that praise which comes easily, especially when its origin is the common multitude. Also, he considers that he has merely done his duty, and is therefore unworthy of praise. He pursues honor as an ideal and expects no other reward.

After Cominius has transacted some business, Coriolanus begs a favor of his general. He recalls that a poor man in Corioli had treated him kindly, but the Romans had taken him prisoner. He asks that the poor man be given his freedom. Of course Cominius agrees, but then Coriolanus cannot remember his name.

> **Comment: This episode shows a hidden aspect of Marcius' character. He wants to do a generous deed, but forgets a most important detail. Generosity does not come naturally to him, despite his kind feelings. This forgetfulness does not mean that Coriolanus does not care about the man he says he wants to help. He is so wrapped up in himself and his own affairs that, like so many self-centered people, he forgets the name of someone to whom he has been introduced.**

Summary: The entire scene is occupied with further revelation of the character of Caius Marcius Coriolanus.

1. The valiant soldier refuses a princely portion of the booty in recognition of his bravery, taking instead a war horse, and what is more important, the title Coriolanus.

2. His acceptance of these two relatively small gifts in terms of monetary value reveals his pride in personal honor, not economic aggrandisement.

3. He cannot bear to hear himself praised, another aspect of his pride in himself.

4. The **episode** of the poor man in Corioli reveals Caius Marcius' self-centered nature, and shows that generous actions do not come naturally to him.

ACT I: SCENE X

This last scene of Act I takes place in the camp of the Volsces. Aufidius, bleeding from battle, enters with a few soldiers. He is distraught and depressed because Corioli has been taken, and although the Romans will return it after suitable peace negotiations, Aufidius' pride is hurt. He has now been beaten five different times by Caius Marcius and is beginning to think this will always be the case. In defeat Aufidius is less noble and valiant than he has seemed before. He now speaks rather meanly of the way in which he will be revenged on Caius Marcius by the use of craft, even if Marcius were a guest in his own house. Instead of generously respecting his opponent's prowess, Aufidius now actively hates him.

Comment: This scene contrasts with the triumph of Coriolanus and informs the audience of the bitter, treacherous side of Aufidius' nature. It also points ahead to the conspiratorial conclusion of the play.

Summary: This first act is an excellent example of dramatic exposition, conveying information and introducing characters in a functional manner.

1. We meet all the principal characters and their interrelationships are shown. The most important relationships are:

    (a) Caius Marcius and his wife, Virgilia

    (b) Caius Marcius and his mother, Volumnia

    (c) Caius Marcius and his chief military rival, Aufidius

(d) Caius Marcius and his chief political rivals, Sicinius Veleutus and Junius Brutus, the tribunes of the people.

2. The brilliance of Caius Marcius as a soldier is shown. He is a superbly effective warrior, despite the fact that he is rather too proud of his own honor.

3. The political incapacity of Caius Marcius is hinted at in his verbal attacks on the common people as well as on his troops.

4. The basic political conflict, the dispute between the patricians and the plebeians, is introduced and explained.

CORIOLANUS

TEXTUAL ANALYSIS

ACT II

ACT II: SCENE I

If the last act was mainly one of **exposition**, largely devoted to showing Caius Marcius Coriolanus as a soldier, this act shows Caius Marcius the triumphant warrior and the unsuccessful politician. Act II is mainly political.

The scene is a public place in Rome, and Menenius enters with the two tribunes, Sicinius and Brutus. They await news from the battlefront, and Menenius remarks that the common people will be unhappy to hear of Caius Marcius' success since they dislike him so much. Sicinius says that nature teaches beasts to know their friends, a remark which seems to indicate unexpected dislike for the commons from one of their representatives. Brutus and Menenius then engage in a witty exchange about Coriolanus, but then the patrician goes on to ask, in a characteristically ironic way, whether there is any vice in which Caius Marcius is weak and which the tribunes do not possess in abundance. Brutus claims that Caius Marcius has all possible vices, and Sicinius returns to Marcius' pride above all else, and Brutus speaks of his boasting. Menenius then turns the tables on the two tribunes by asking them if they know what people think of them in the city, and then telling them that they really have no right to call Marcius proud. They ought to look at themselves to see a pair of meritless, proud, perpetually angry magistrates, in other words, fools.

The tribunes are a trifle taken aback and try to retaliate in kind, claiming that Menenius himself is known quite well in the city for what he really is. But Menenius is too quick for them and he seizes the advantage by giving a character sketch of himself as a "humorous (whimsical) patrician" who likes to drink his hot wine straight and whose judicial weakness is taking the side of the first person to see him about a complaint. Sometimes too he is a trifle hasty about minor things and he loves night life. But his worst fault, as he sees it, is his uncompromising frankness. Rather than do anything underhanded he lets his dislike be known in his speech. He now rounds on the tribunes and tells them, quite frankly of course, that they are no Lycurguses.

Comment: Lycurgus was the famous Spartan lawgiver of the ninth century B.C.

In addition they are not good statesmen and have put their case badly: in fact they have sounded like a pair of asses most of the time. Since they are the people's representatives he must put up with them, but he cannot say they have good faces, a deliberately ambiguous remark: (1) virtuous faces which bespeak virtuous hearts; (2) handsome faces. Now if the tribunes can see such faults in him, then what can their blinded eyesight see in their own characters?

Brutus, overwhelmed by this flow of words, simply stammers "We know you well enough," but again Menenius seizes the advantage and says that the tribunes have never known anything, neither themselves nor anyone else. He sees them as ambitious for the respect, the uncapping and the bowing of poor men. They love to exercise their tiny bit of authority, spending a whole morning on a trivial case, and then adjourning another. They worry more about their personal comfort than about the administration of justice, and if they should get a stomach ache they raise a great cry and adjourn the lawsuit.

At last Brutus manages to get in a gibe and claims that Menenius is better known for his wit at a banquet than for his ability as a judge in the Capitol. But again Menenius lets fly: the speech of the tribunes is worthless, yet they claim that Caius Marcius is proud when he is worth the sum total of all the tribunes' ancestors since the legendary great flood. He disgustedly bids them farewell as "herdsmen of the beastly plebeians."

Comment: Menenius shows his quick wit as a debater here, and also his own contempt for the common people. His use of the word "herdsmen" indicates that he sees the common people as a flock of mindless sheep, or something worse. In addition, Shakespeare uses Menenius to give an opinion on the tribunes, something that will make us look rather closely at their conduct in the future.

Volumnia, Virgilia, and Valeria then enter to greet Menenius, who is now alone. The mother greets him with the news that Marcius is on his way home, having sent letters to her, to the Senate, to Virgilia, and, she thinks, to Menenius. The old patrician almost goes into an ecstasy of joy and says he will hold a feast. He enquires whether Marcius is wounded, as is customary with him. Virgilia fearfully protests, but Volumnia joyously announces that indeed he is, and that he is returning for the third time with the oak garland for having saved the life of a Roman citizen in battle. Further, he has beaten Aufidius again. Menenius rejoices and asks whether the Senate has been informed, and Volumnia says that the general has written to them and praised Marcius most highly. As Valeria says, "wondrous things" are spoken of him. Virgilia hopes they are true, but Volumnia interrupts with an exclamation of disgust. Of course they're true.

Again Menenius enquires after the wounds of Caius Marcius, and Volumnia says that he is wounded in the shoulder and the left arm. As a result he will have great scars to show the people when he becomes a candidate for public office. He now has a total of twenty-seven different wounds received in all his war expeditions, each one of which, says Menenius, meant death to an enemy.

Comment: This preoccupation with wounds is really political. It was customary for candidates for political office to stand poorly dressed in the market place for a given length of time to solicit votes from the people by showing their wounds as evidence of their deserving. These scars would indicate the worthiness of the man in terms of what he had already done in the physical defense of Rome. Presumably, such a man would make an excellent representative of justice. By even mentioning the matter, Volumnia shows that she now has a political as well as a military career in mind for her son.

At this moment the trumpets sound and Cominius and Titus Lartius, the Roman generals, enter, followed by Coriolanus, wearing the oak leaf garland, with a train of soldiers behind him. A herald announces the new title of Coriolanus in virtue of his valor inside the gates of Corioli. Everyone rejoices, but again Coriolanus rejects empty praise, and as soon as he sees his mother he kneels before her in respect. He has done what she would have wished him to do in battle. This kneeling is very important because in the last act Volumnia kneels to her son in a totally different situation. Coriolanus then addresses himself to Virgilia as "My gracious silence, hail" and he chides her for appearing as sad as the widows of Corioli.

Comment: In this short speech Coriolanus describes his wife and then asks if she would have laughed had he been killed, since she weeps at his triumph. This is the first indication we have of any deep feeling between the warrior and his wife. It is also a most penetrating character study of Virgilia.

Volumnia and Menenius interrupt this tender interlude with rejoicing and Coriolanus says he must visit the patricians to thank them for his promotion. Volumnia joyfully proclaims that she has seen all but one of her wishes fulfilled in Coriolanus - and she has hopes of the last.

Comment: This remark of course refers to political office, though Volumnia does not specifically say so.

As they set off for the Capitol, Sicinius and Brutus enter to tell of the tumultuous reception Coriolanus is receiving from all ranks and conditions of people. The tribunes are therefore most unhappy, and Sicinius fears that Marcius will be elected Consul, one of Rome's two chief magistrates. Brutus tacitly agrees, and says he fears that during his term of office (which would be one year) the power of the tribunes may be weakened, if not altogether destroyed. Sicinius suggests that since Coriolanus cannot bear his honors without showing his contempt for the populace, he will be unsuccessful in his candidacy and will lose public regard. If the tribunes work hard on recalling the old hostility between the commons and Coriolanus, the people will probably forget his services to the state. Brutus, musing aloud, remembers that Coriolanus had once said that if he were to stand for Consul he would never go through with the custom of standing in the market place in humble clothes, showing his wounds to the people to ask their approval.

Comment: The office of Consul was not elective in the modern sense, but the people had the right to approve or disapprove of a candidate. This they did by giving their verbal opinion. Note here how Brutus uses Marcius' own attitudes concerning the common people, though in some respects the tribune himself despises the people he can so easily lead.

Brutus gives his opinion that Coriolanus would sooner miss out on the office if he could not gain it merely by the request of the gentry. The two tribunes, of course, wish nothing better than that Coriolanus should keep to that particular policy. They then start thinking about strategy, and Brutus suggests that they recall Coriolanus' hostility to the people and his desire to treat them like beasts of burden, taking away all their political rights. Sicinius heartily agrees, and remarks that they should suggest these things when Coriolanus will have made the people angry at him, something that is sure to happen. At this moment a messenger arrives to summon the tribunes to the Capitol. He confirms the tribunes' suspicions by saying that everyone now expects Caius Marcius to be Consul, and adds that his valor has everyone at his feet. The tribunes leave.

Summary: This scene is important for its development of the political **theme** of the play.

1. It shows the adulation that the people of Rome give to their hero, Caius Marcius Coriolanus.

2. Volumnia shows her political ambitions for her son in thinking of his standing for public office.

3. The characters of the two tribunes, Sicinius and Brutus, are further revealed. They are wily political plotters and do not really seem to be true patriots because they are more concerned about their own power than the welfare of the people. They seem to despise the very crowd they lead.

4. Menenius gives us the aristocrats' opinion of the tribunes, so that we now have both sides. Throughout the rest of the act their plotting seems to show that his comments are justified.

5. In his greeting to Virgilia, Coriolanus reveals a softer, more loving aspect of his nature.

6. Coriolanus again shows himself incapable of receiving praise.

ACT II: SCENE II

This scene takes place within the Capitol where two officers, who are laying cushions for the senators, are discussing the selection of a Consul. Apparently there are three candidates, but the Second Officer seems fairly sure that Coriolanus will be the successful one. The First Officer recalls his pride and dislike of the common people, but the Second Officer says that he's not the first who hasn't loved them, but out of his noble indifference to public opinion he has let the people see his attitude. The First Officer notes that Coriolanus seems to seek their hate rather unwisely, but the Second Officer declares that he has deserved so much recognition from his country that it would be an act of ingratitude to deny him this Office.

Comment: Throughout Shakespeare it is important to note the comments of ordinary people. They generally represent unedited public opinion. Here, for instance, the two officers give the principal reason for approving Coriolanus' appointment - a refusal would be an act of ingratitude.

At that instant there is a flourish of trumpets and the entire senate enters. Sicinius and Brutus, as the tribunes of the people, are present, though they sit separately. Menenius opens the proceedings by announcing that the Senate has sent for Titus Lartius, who had been left to administer Corioli. He then asks Cominius, the present Consul, to speak of the valorous deeds of Caius Marcius Coriolanus. A senator seconds the request and asks the support of the tribunes in influencing the people to ratify the Senate's decision. Sicinius answers civilly, but Brutus declares that Coriolanus will need to value the common people a little more than he has done in the past. Menenius, rather embarrassed, rules Brutus out of order, but the tribune presses the point. In reply Menenius says that Coriolanus doesn't have to act as the "bedfellow to the commons," at which point Coriolanus offers to leave, saying that he can't bear to listen to a recital of his personal exploits. Brutus, with heavy **irony**, hopes that he is not sending Coriolanus away, but the soldier replies that his dislike of praise is sending him away.

Cominius then begins a recital of all of Coriolanus' bold deeds, and here we get a full account of the young man's first battle against the forces of the Tarquins when he was a mere sixteen years old. There he did more than was expected of a grown man, wounding Tarquin himself in the knee, and obtaining the first of his oak leaf garlands.

Comment: Here Shakespeare is more definite than Plutarch, who refers to Coriolanus as a "stripling" in his first battle. The Tarquins had been the kings of Rome, but they became tyrants and the Romans rebelled and banished them in 510 B.C. This reference gives us some idea of the age of the historical Coriolanus. His victory at Corioli seems to have been in 493 B.C., and therefore he is approximately thirty three.

Cominius then continues to tell of Coriolanus' gallant exploits at Corioli. Menenius and the senators are overwhelmed by this account of valor, and are even more amazed when Cominius says that Coriolanus would take no reward for his deeds, considering his performance sufficient glory in itself.

Comment: This attitude helps to make *Coriolanus* a true exponent of the Roman virtus, and also a true Renaissance hero in his search for fama, for fame based on personal honor and strength. The kind of reputation a man could leave to posterity was all important, and therefore he should strive to live as virtuously as possible.

Coriolanus is then called for and Menenius announces to him that the Senate has decided to make him Consul. In reply Marcius says that he owes the Senate his life and service. But when Menenius tells him he must stand in the market place to speak to the people Marcius requests that this custom be omitted. Sicinius promptly insists on the people's rights in this matter and says that they will not allow any abridgement of the custom. Menenius tells Coriolanus to go along with the custom, but the new Consul protests that the will be extremely embarrassed, and further, he thinks that the ceremony could well be dispensed with. Brutus notes this comment. Despite the protests of Coriolanus, Menenius insists, and asks the tribunes to speak to the plebeians in favor of the Senate's decision. As the Senate departs, the tribunes comment on Coriolanus' conduct.

Summary: In this scene both the military and political **themes** come together.

1. The valor of Coriolanus is considered sufficient cause to make him Consul - and, after all, the Consul often led the army in time of war.

2. Coriolanus is not a good politician because he does not soften his remarks. He would rather be misunderstood than appear to be untrue to himself.

3. He is once more embarrassed when he hears himself praised, because he believes that no man should be praised for pursuing such essential ideals as duty and honor. For this reason he hates to make his wounds speak for him in the market place.

4. The attitudes of Brutus and Sicinius are again shown. They hate and fear Coriolanus and will work for his downfall.

5. Coriolanus gives the tribunes cause to hate him by suggesting that the right of the common people to approve an appointment should be taken away. Such a suggestion sounds tyrannical.

ACT II: SCENE III

This scene takes place in the Roman Forum, where Coriolanus must stand to ask the approval of the people. Seven or eight citizens enter discussing what they should do when Coriolanus asks for their voices. Four separate attitudes are obvious: (1) the people ought not to deny their approval; (2) the people have the right to withhold their voices if they wish; (3) the people would be ungrateful if they refused to accept the evidence of Coriolanus' many wounds; (4) the people ought to remember Coriolanus' attitude over the corn as well as the fact that he called them a "many-headed multitude."

Comment: This image of a hydra-headed monster is frequently used by *Coriolanus* in reference to the Roman citizens. It refers to the Lernean hydra, a water monster with somewhere between nine and fifty heads. Each time one head was cut off two more grew in its place. Its destruction was one of the labors of Hercules. There is an implicit and explicit comparison between Coriolanus and Hercules throughout the play.

Finally, after more discussion, the Third Citizen comments that if only he would lean a little toward the people, Coriolanus would be a worthy man.

Coriolanus then enters in the garb of humility, accompanied by Menenius, who warns him to be mild. The Third Citizen in the meantime has told his followers to come up to Coriolanus in twos and threes so that he will have to make his request for voices to specific persons. Coriolanus still protests to Menenius; how can he ask his wounds to speak for him when he really wants to say that the citizen-soldiery had run away from the same battle in which he had distinguished himself. Menenius begs him to be temperate, but Coriolanus in reply tells him to make the people wash their faces and clean their teeth.

Three citizens then enter, a "brace" as Coriolanus calls them, using a term used for game birds and animals rather than people. He cannot humble himself and claims that his worth and not his wish has brought him to the market place to ask for voices. When the First Citizen says that he must ask kindly for the office, Coriolanus goes through the motions of doing so. But he does not show his wounds, saying that he'll do so in private. The first two citizens give their voices, but the Second Citizen is a trifle dubious. The Fourth Citizen claims that Coriolanus has not always deserved nobly of his country because he has not loved the common people, even though he has been successful in war. In reply Coriolanus argues that his refusal to be "common" in his love is really a recommendation, but if the people desire, he will take off his cap to them, and so he asks for their voices. The Third and Fourth Citizens gladly give their approval, but Coriolanus again avoids showing his wounds. As the group departs, he grumbles against the custom of begging from the plebeians. He would rather not have the position than do so, but he will continue since he is half-way through the business.

Three more citizens appear and Coriolanus asks for their voices after speaking of his wounds and his battles. Again he does not actually show his wounds, and his rage at his humiliation is barely suppressed.

Immediately after, Menenius, accompanied by the tribunes, enters and says that Coriolanus has stood in the market place as long as the custom requires and he can now go. Sicinius and Brutus have also given their approval, which is of course that of the people. Coriolanus can hardly wait to get out of his humble clothes and the two patricians arrange to meet at the Senate.

Left alone, Sicinius and Brutus await the arrival of the people, and they speak of the pride with which Coriolanus wore his humble garments and begged voices. The plebeians then come in and the tribunes ask if they have given their voices. They say that they have, but express misgivings: Coriolanus seemed to be mocking the people when he asked for their voices; he didn't actually show his wounds, his manner seemed insulting. Sicinius seizes on these comments and says that the people were very foolish to have approved under such circumstances. Brutus agrees and asks why on earth the plebeians didn't do as they were told. After all, Coriolanus has always been their enemy, even when he lacked power; what will he do now that he has power, since he has always opposed the political rights and liberties of the plebeians? Sicinius suggests that they should have extorted a promise of support from him as their price; then Coriolanus would probably have become angry and they could legitimately have refused him. Brutus builds on his suggestion and harps on the fact that Coriolanus mocked them even as he asked their support, and Sicinius feigns amazement that the plebeians gave their voices under such circumstances. The Third Citizen says that since the appointment is not yet confirmed the plebeians can still revoke their voices; the First and Second

Citizens agree and claim that they can raise a thousand voices hostile to Coriolanus.

Sicinius and Brutus then give the citizens a list of the arguments they should use in raising this opposition: say that the people have chosen a Consul who will take away their civil liberties; emphasize the pride of Coriolanus, his contempt for the people, and especially the mockery with which he asked for their voices. Then, with a political master stroke, Brutus suggests that the three citizens blame the tribunes for agreeing to the appointment of Coriolanus. Sicinius picks up the argument, telling them to say that they agreed because of the insistence of the tribunes, while Brutus adds specific detail saying that the tribunes had told the people of Coriolanus' past valor and noble lineage.

> **Comment: Here Shakespeare lists the lineage of Coriolanus and gets very confused. He lists as ancestors some who lived after Coriolanus: Censorinus (Censor in 265 B.C.), and Publius and Quintus Marcius, the aqueduct builders of 139 B.C. At any rate, Caius Marcius did come of a noble line. The confusion seems to come from Shakespeare's failure to check his source carefully.**

Sicinius repeats Brutus' argument and says that the people now ought to claim that they have discovered from Coriolanus' current behavior and from recollecting his past attitudes that the new Consul is an enemy of the people. Therefore they wish to revoke their approval. Again Brutus repeats the same argument and suggests that when a sufficient crowd has been gathered the citizens ought to go to the Capitol. The people agree enthusiastically and depart to carry out the plan.

Brutus and Sicinius remain behind to contemplate their handiwork, Brutus remarking that this new mutiny will so provoke the anger of Coriolanus that he will reveal himself in his true colors. Sicinius, with an eye for appearances, suggests that the two of them ought to hasten to the Senate so that they will arrive before the crowd. In this way the revocation will seem to be wholly the idea of the populace, and not instigated by the tribunes.

Comment: The role of Brutus and Sicinius in this scene is completely duplicitous (two-faced). They have not been shown as actively supporting the candidacy of Coriolanus, but they are skilled now at pretending that they did so. They are playing both the patricians and plebeians against each other, and they seem to be doing so for their own personal ends. Shrewdly, they manage to keep on the right side of both groups by making the riot appear to be the spontaneous idea of the people. Note the way the tribunes hammer away at a couple of basic points, obviously believing that there is strength in repetition.

Summary: This scene is important for its revelation of the real nature of politics and political plotting.

1. Coriolanus strives to put on the "correct" face for the occasion in pleading for the voices of the people. Unfortunately for him he is too stiffnecked, or perhaps too honest, to flatter where he does not love.

2. The comments of the citizens reveal differing attitudes toward Coriolanus, but yet the commoners are easily led by whoever seems the strongest personality around at the time. In some ways the **metaphor** of "hydra-

headed monster" is correct because the mob is fickle and frequently changes its collective mind to the danger of the state.

3. The plotting of Sicinius and Brutus reveals the tribunes as practiced political maneuverers who seem more interested in themselves and their power than in the good of the people they are supposed to represent. There is some **irony** in the complaint that Coriolanus does not love the common people when we see the way the people's representatives act toward their own. The chief motive of the tribunes seems to be fear and hatred of Coriolanus.

ACT III: SCENE I

This act opens in a Roman street to the sound of cornets as Coriolanus, Menenius, the nobility, Cominius, Titus Lartius, and some senators enter. Titus Lartius informs Coriolanus that since Tullus Aufidius had raised another force against Rome a speedy agreement had been concluded in Corioli. Coriolanus seems disappointed that the Volscians have not been totally crushed and thinks it a matter of time until they rise again. Cominius disagrees and doesn't think Rome will have any further trouble from them in the current generation. Titus, in answer to a question by Coriolanus, says that Aufidius was angry at his followers for surrendering the town in such a cowardly manner. In addition, Aufidius had spoken of his rivalry with Coriolanus and his hatred toward Rome. He has now retired to his town of Antium, and Coriolanus wishes he could find an excuse to meet him there.

Comment: This short interlude serves to recall Coriolanus' skill as a warrior and it also helps to reveal the character of Aufidius. In some respects Shakespeare does not fully succeed with this figure; he is supposed to be noble and generous, yet also meanminded, and at the same time he must be an adequate foil character to Coriolanus. Perhaps he is made to bear too much weight.

Sicinius and Brutus now enter, and Coriolanus says how much he despises them as the "tongues o'the'common mouth."

Comment: Note the implicit image of the people as a human body. By extension, the state is also included in the same image. It will become more important throughout this act.

The tribunes warn the troop of patricians, and Coriolanus in particular, not to proceed any further, because the new Consul has not received the approval of the people. Coriolanus promptly blusters "Have I had children's voices?" The senators wish to force a passage to the market place, but the tribunes advise against this policy, claiming that the people are so enraged that it would provoke open battle. Coriolanus then turns on the tribunes asking what is the matter with their "herd" if they can now disclaim what their tongues had just spoken. He asks rather shrewdly whether the tribunes might not have led the people on, and disregarding Menenius' warnings to keep calm, he claims that the tribunes are here plotting to circumvent the wishes of the nobility. If such a limitation is permitted, Coriolanus sees Rome as actually being ruled by a mob who cannot and will not be ruled by their betters.

Comment: This statement is another manifestation of a fairly common attitude in Shakespeare's day. In general, members of the middle and upper classes opposed any weakening of the central government, seeing the mob as so untrustworthy that it could not be given political power. To allow the mob to dictate would be a species of anarchy, and chaos would result. This play seems to give some justification for this low opinion of the mob.

Brutus promptly returns to the root of the argument: Coriolanus' opposition to giving free corn to the people and his attack on those who had supported their cause.

Comment: In Act I the complaint had been against giving the people corn at their own price, but this is the first time that free corn has been mentioned. Shakespeare has changed his source here, because Plutarch places this incident after the people have refused Marcius as Consul. Two insurrections have been combined in Act I.

Sicinius then adopts a fatherly tone and suggests that Coriolanus should be humbler and gentler to the people. Menenius tries to calm everyone down, and Cominius tries to act as a moderate voice, saying that Coriolanus has not really deserved this insult from the people. Coriolanus, however, is not to be stopped. He offers to make exactly the same speech against free corn once more. He won't beg pardon of the changeable, smelly crowd because he would rather they regarded him as honest enough not to flatter. He is opposed to making peace with the people on this matter of the consul's office. Giving in would encourage the weed of rebellion to grow in the state which the nobles have so carefully cultivated.

Comment: This image of the state as a well-tended garden or field is frequent in Shakespeare, most notably in Richard II.

One of the senators now tries to silence Coriolanus, but it is impossible. He will not be stopped and goes on to say that he would be untrue to his valor if by his silence he permitted the spread of "those measles [leprosy]," that hidden disease in the otherwise healthy state.

Comment: Here is the image of rebellion as a disease in the healthy, well-ordered state. The nobility are in the position of doctors here. Again we have the image of the state as a human body which needs careful tending and medication.

By now Coriolanus is in a full-blown rage and he insults the tribunes. But what really angers him beyond all measure is the comment of Sicinius that the mind of the new consul "shall remain a poison where it is" and not corrupt anything else. This imperative shall is of course totally disrespectful to the nobles, and Coriolanus sees red. He calls Sicinius the leader of a bunch of minnows and tries to show the patricians their folly in granting any political power to the mob. He rages on and warns that chaos can be the only result when two authorities, each equal in rank, attempt to rule the state.

Then he returns to the matter of the free corn and blames all the later trouble in the state on the weakness of the Senate in acceding to the demands of the mutinous mob on that occasion. And again he attacks the populace, claiming that they deserve nothing because of their cowardice in battle. They spend more time and energy in mutiny against their leaders than in fighting the enemy. As Coriolanus sees things, the Senate ought not be courteous to the populace unless it intends to lose its own authority. After all, the populace is in the majority and is likely to insist on the rights of mere numbers. The result would be the overturning of the established order, and crows would peck at eagles.

Comment: Remember that the eagle was the symbol of imperial Rome, and in addition it is supposed to be the king of birds because it flies the highest. The image that Coriolanus uses is therefore one of overturned authority in which a bird that feeds on carrion, the crow, can attack the monarch of birds. This stands for what would happen if the Senate were to abdicate its power to the populace.

Obviously Coriolanus continually speaks for the aristocratic ideal of government, not a democratic one. This fact has helped to make this play unpopular. But as the action progresses we are forced to see that rule by power-seeking demagogues who manipulate the mob is not a good substitute for the government by the elite that Coriolanus wants. In addition, he fears divided authority.

Coriolanus continues to plead with the senators to get rid of the voice of the populace and to rule them as members of the state who don't really know what is good for themselves. He supports the principle that the integrity of the senators is worth preserving even at the risk of abolishing all the political representation of the populace. Such a remedy is strong medicine for the body politic, but the senators should not hesitate to administer it for the health of the state.

Sicinius explodes at this series of comments and says that since Coriolanus has spoken like a traitor he shall be forced to answer as a traitor. Note that imperative again. The tribunes are indeed exceeding their authority. Then Sicinius calls for an aedile to come to arrest Coriolanus as a traitor to the state.

Comment: The aediles were instituted at the same time as the tribunes of the people and seem to have been subordinate to them, acting as their assistants, as a kind of police force. Incidentally, Shakespeare has again changed his source by speeding up events for dramatic effect.

Sicinius repeats his charge of traitor and lays hands on Coriolanus who calls him an "old goat." The patricians promise to pledge themselves for Coriolanus, but more aediles enter with a group of citizens. The plebeians call for Coriolanus' destruction and the senators vainly try to restore order. Sicinius then addresses the mob, claiming that Caius Marcius desires to take away the people's liberties. Menenius remonstrates with him for inflaming the passions of the mob instead of trying to quench them, but Sicinius speaks for government by the many: "What is the city but the people?" This sentiment meets with support from the multitude, who give the tribunes their vote of confidence. Cominius claims that this kind of divisive attitude is the way to destroy the city physically and politically, but by now Sicinius and Brutus are really playing upon the fickle mob and Sicinius calls for Caius Marcius to be taken to the Tarpeian Rock.

Comment: The Tarpeian Rock was a precipice situated on the Capitoline Hill in ancient Rome. From there persons convicted of treason were thrown to their death.

Menenius tries to temporize once more, Brutus calls on the crowd to arrest Coriolanus, who draws his sword, and all is confusion. Again Menenius calls for order and asks the nobles to help Coriolanus. This they do and the people are driven off.

Comment: The moderate words of Menenius do absolutely no good in terms of pacifying the Roman populace. Coriolanus has to draw his sword before anything is accomplished. As a result he is proved right in his allegation that the people must be treated roughly, almost like animals, before they can be made to understand or be controlled. There is also an ironic parallel with the situation of Coriolanus' death in the last act where the drawing of his sword proves fatal to him.

Menenius immediately tells Coriolanus to flee, but naturally he wants to stay and fight. A senator, however, supports Menenius, and finally Cominius adds his voice. Protesting that he could beat forty of the populace at once, Coriolanus is at last persuaded to leave while the politicians are left behind to treat the sore of rebellion. Note again the image of disease for the condition of the state.

Left alone with Menenius, a patrician regrets Coriolanus' policy, but Menenius pleads in extenuation that Coriolanus is too noble and too honest to flatter anyone for anything. Further, he is accustomed to speaking his mind frankly. Nevertheless, even Menenius wishes that he had spoken more gently to the people.

The tribunes, together with the rabble, now return and call again for Coriolanus' blood. A citizen, speaking for all, claims that as the tribunes are the mouths of the people so the citizens are the tribunes' hands, and therefore they wish to cast Caius Marcius from the Tarpeian Rock for his treason. Menenius tries to calm them down, but the tribunes continually inflame the mob. A debate then ensues between Menenius and Sicinius. Menenius claims that to destroy such a man as Coriolanus would be an act of ingratitude, but Sicinius claims he is a disease which must be cut out of the body politic. Menenius counters by saying that he is simply a diseased limb that needs treatment rather than possibly fatal amputation. The tribunes are not to be convinced because they see Coriolanus as a gangrened foot, and Brutus says that he must be cut off to halt the spread of the disease.

Comment: Again the state is seen as analogous to the human body - even by the tribunes and the citizen-rabble.

Menenius warns of the dangers of civil war and destruction if the tribunes follow their proposed course, and suggests that they proceed according to the established rules of legal practice. He promises that Coriolanus will appear at a properly constituted legal trial. At this point the tribunes, somewhat mollified, order the people to lay down their swords, but threaten open war if Caius Marcius fails to appear.

Summary: This scene is an important turning point in the political action of the play. From now on the action turns against Coriolanus. No longer is he the spotless military hero.

1. The tribunes inflame the people and play upon their fears that they will lose political power. We, however, can wonder about the mixed motives of the tribunes.

2. In trying to order the senators around, the tribunes exceed their authority.

3. The mob's insistence on condemning Coriolanus without a fair trial shows that he is right in his claim that government by the populace breeds anarchy and disorder. The only justice the mob understands is that of physical violence.

4. Caius Marcius shows himself a staunch supporter of a centralized, aristocratic system of government. In other words, the status quo. Unbridled rule by the people and consequent division of authority breed chaos.

5. Menenius shows that moderation is really rather ineffective as a method of bringing about order. He manages to succeed, but the risk of failure is great. Not until the rabble fears the use of force do things calm down.

6. The entire scene shows the populace in the worst possible light, and while Coriolanus is not right in his own behavior, his attitude is in some ways preferable because it is aimed at preserving some semblance of peace and order in the state. One of the difficulties of this play is that while the hero's opinions and attitudes cannot be fully accepted, neither can those of anyone else, and Caius Marcius is in some ways more honest than all the rest.

ACT III: SCENE II

This scene takes place in a room of Coriolanus' house and is concerned with attempts to make him see political reason. Caius Marcius enters, still in a rage, and claims that he will stand firm against any kind of torture the mob may propose.

One noble agrees with him, but Coriolanus is puzzled that Volumnia, his mother, who had never said anything good of the populace, seems to disapprove of his action. Just at this moment she enters, and Coriolanus asks why she wishes he had acted more mildly. Here Volumnia shows a more astute political sense than that of her son; she wishes he had made more certain of his power before he attempted to exercise it so openly. Again, Coriolanus is amazed, but Volumnia says that he acted too soon. He should have waited until the people were powerless to cross him. Menenius and a senator support Volumnia's plea for moderation as she goes on to say that she hates the idea of apologizing to the people and begging their help as much as he does. Nevertheless, her intellect tells her that at the moment this is good policy.

> **Comment: From Coriolanus' opening remark concerning his Mother's detestation of the common people we can easily see where his own contempt was nurtured. We must remember too that Volumnia has long been a widow and has carefully brought up her son to act only from the noblest, most aristocratic, and most Roman of motives. This side of Volumnia is not shown us in Plutarch, where Caius Marcius' education is criticized for its severe limitations because he was brought up by a woman. Shakespeare, however, has chosen to emphasize the unusually close relationship between mother and son as part of the motivation for some of Coriolanus' actions.**

The suggestion of admitting to the people that he had been wrong galls Coriolanus, who says that he couldn't bring himself to apologize to the gods, therefore how can he apologize to the people. Again, Volumnia tries to tell him that he is too inflexible, and uses one of his own arguments: since honor and policy grow together in time of war, in this case he must grant that they should also work together. Coriolanus at first refuses to listen, but she goes on with an analogy; it is no more dishonorable to talk kindly to the mob than it is to capture a town with fair words to save the lives of his soldiers. She herself would certainly dissemble in this case because the end is good, the preservation of the internal peace and stable government of the city of Rome. Menenius naturally agrees with this argument from expediency, and so she goes on to tell Coriolanus that he should take off his hat to the people, and even kneel before them. He must be as humble as a ripe mulberry; in other words a ripe mulberry is easily bruised with the touch and he must be extremely soft in his appearance and manner. Then, when he has the attention of the people he should say that since he has been brought up as a soldier he simply doesn't have the honeyed words they are accustomed to hear. Then, of course, he must say that he will arrange his behavior so that it will please them. Volumnia almost orders Coriolanus to do as she suggests, despite his dislike of flattering anyone.

Cominius then arrives with the news that people are expressing their anger against Coriolanus in the market place, and suggests that he had better come with a strong force or make a good case for himself. The consensus is that fair speech is the only answer. But Coriolanus protests that he cannot act as his mother suggests because it is totally against his nature. Volumnia then appeals to his affections, as she later does in Act V, saying that she made him a soldier through her praises, and now he must perform a new role, even if it is foreign to him. Coriolanus is shocked by the suggestion that he must prostitute himself to the people in order to achieve office, and he refuses. At this point Volumnia castigates him openly, telling him to do just as he pleases and let Rome go to ruin. She denies cowardice in herself and takes responsibility for his valor, but says that his pride comes completely from himself. She has no part of such dangerous obstinacy. Almost immediately, Coriolanus backs down. He cannot bear his mother's contempt because her good opinion is all-important to him. Therefore he agrees to go to the market place and insinuate himself into the love of the people by artful speeches. He sends greetings to Virgilia, and says that he will return as Consul or never trust his tongue in flattery again. With a curt "Do your will" Volumnia leaves. Significantly, the last lines of the scene show Coriolanus echoing Menenius' advice - "Mildly!" This is to be the watchword for the next scene.

Summary: This scene is important for the way in which it shows up the relationship between Volumnia and her son.

1. Volumnia is more expedient and more politically minded than Coriolanus. She sees that the end can justify the means and that at times one must dissemble for a worthy purpose.

2. Coriolanus is too inflexible in his behavior and even arguments based on affection are insufficient. Volumnia must become angry with him and show her contempt before he will budge.

3. For Coriolanus, his mother's contempt is more than he can stand, chiefly because throughout his life she has been the source of all his knowledge of honor and virtue.

4. On the insistence of Volumnia, backed up by Cominius and Menenius, Coriolanus agrees to close his eyes to his principles temporarily and dissemble to the people in the market place.

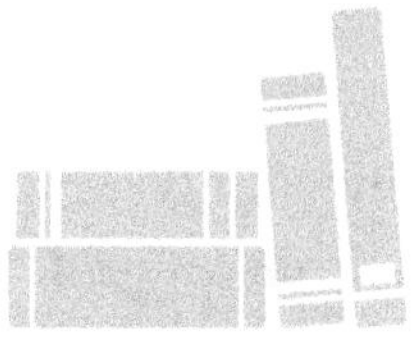

CORIOLANUS

TEXTUAL ANALYSIS

ACT III

ACT III: SCENE III

The scene now returns to the Roman forum. Sicinius and Brutus enter and Brutus suggests that Coriolanus be charged with a desire to gain tyrannical power over the people. But if he should wriggle out of that charge they should accuse him of hating the people, and claim in addition that the booty captured during the war with the Antiates was never distributed. They are planning here to charge Coriolanus with deliberate dishonesty, and by having all their charges ready they are trying to nullify the legal process under which they have agreed to try him.

An aedile then brings the news that Coriolanus is coming, accompanied by Menenius and some of the senators who have always been in his favor. Sicinius then asks whether a voting list of those against Caius Marcius has been prepared, and he arranges that the people will follow whatever he says in terms of passing sentence on Coriolanus. They will repeat his pronouncement of fine or death, and support the truth of the charges. Brutus then tells the aedile to make sure that the noise will continue so that the people will insist upon immediate execution of whatever sentence the tribunes decree. As the aedile leaves, Brutus says that the first thing to do will be to anger Coriolanus. Once enraged, he will be incapable of controlling his tongue and will let his true self be shown. Thus he will play into the hands of the tribunes and bring about his own destruction.

Comment: The opening portion of this scene shows Shakespeare at his best in his understanding of the nature of politics and underhanded means of exercising political power. The stagemanaging techniques used by the two ambitious and demagogic tribunes are not outmoded even now. The way in which totalitarian governments still arrange "spontaneous" outbursts of rioting or enthusiasm is markedly similar to the methods employed by the tribunes. Shakespeare is here dealing with what we may term Realpolitik, based on the acquisition of power by the power hungry.

At this point Coriolanus, Menenius, Cominius and others arrive, Menenius all the while counseling calmness. Coriolanus rather bitterly agrees to act as though he were the poorest stable boy in an inn. After all, the end is the preservation of peace and justice in Rome.

The two groups then confront each other, and the aedile gathers in the people to listen to the exchange. The audience is most probably hand-picked, to judge from what has gone before. First Coriolanus asks whether everything is to be settled right at this time and place. Sicinius doesn't really answer the question and demands that Coriolanus here submit himself to the judgment of the people after the charges have been heard. Caius Marcius agrees.

Menenius then takes over and asks the people to consider the wounds Coriolanus has received in battle against the foes of Rome, something the young man laughs off as a collection of mere trifles. In addition, the patrician says that Coriolanus is trained as a warrior, not as an orator or wordspinner, and therefore he sounds more brusque than he really is. Coriolanus then interrupts and asks what is the matter: since once having been accorded the approval of the populace he is now dishonored by its retraction.

> **Comment: These are hardly humble words, and they indicate once more the preoccupation of Coriolanus with his personal honor.**

Sicinius promptly rules Coriolanus out of order and says that the tribunes will do all the questioning. Coriolanus apologizes, and Sicinius charges him with conniving to abolish established political offices in Rome and become the wielder of tyrannical power. For this allegation, which Sicinius seems to accept as proven, he calls Coriolanus a traitor. This word gets under Coriolanus' skin and he repeats it, asking for further details. Menenius counsels calmness, but it is no use. Coriolanus has fallen completely into the trap baited by the astute, and dishonest, tribunes. He is angry, and immediately consigns the entire populace to "The fires i'th'lowest hell," and accuses the tribune of lying.

Without delay Sicinius appeals to the people, who yell "To th' Rock." Sicinius then sums up the case, laying emphasis on Caius Marcius' contemptuous attitude toward the people in the past, and also on his current defiance of the legally constituted judges, the tribunes who are there to try him. Thus Sicinius calls for the "extremest death," but Brutus here interrupts and for the record pleads Coriolanus' services to Rome. This is a very shrewd move, for Coriolanus knows how to deal with insolence and defiance, but not with what would at first appear to be pity and sympathy, especially from inferiors. Thoroughly enraged now, Coriolanus challenges the people to pronounce the penalty of execution by means of the Tarpeian Rock, or banishment. Whatever they want, he will not lower himself one jot in order to plead for mercy from those he despises.

Again Sicinius sums up, and pronounces sentence. Since Coriolanus has hated the common people and has sought to remove their political power, and since he has physically attacked those whose duty it is to dispense justice, his sentence is to be perpetual banishment from Rome under penalty of execution as a traitor should he return. This decision is, of course, ratified by the voices of the populace as the tribunes had planned. Cominius tries to speak for Coriolanus and starts by pleading his own wounds and service, but the tribunes cut off all discussion.

They cannot, however, prevent Caius Marcius Coriolanus from having just about the last word. With scathing contempt he goes further than merely accepting the sentence of the populace. Instead he expresses his hatred of the people as a common pack of mongrel dogs with foul breaths. With superb pride he announces "I banish you." He claims that he doesn't wish to remain in a city filled with such a fickle, rumor-ridden mob. He wishes the ultimate doom upon the city that, not perceiving the mob as its real enemy, will banish its defenders. May Rome be captured without defense by another nation. Then he proudly announces that Rome is not everything, "There is a world elsewhere."

Comment: The much-discussed pride of Coriolanus is shown most notably in this incident. He must have the last word because it would go against his grain to be banished by the populace and remain passive. Hence, he must take the initiative and banish Rome himself. He cannot accept the sentence of lesser people than he. Coriolanus can never admit the fact that he himself could be wrong in his behavior, but yet the conduct of the mob under the tutelage of the tribunes indicates that some of his attitudes towards the populace may have some truth behind them. But, as in all political situations, it is no good being right if you can do nothing about things, and so Coriolanus in his stiffnecked pursuit of the ideal of personal honor cuts himself off from the chance of doing any good at all for Rome. In what seems almost an immature outburst of rage he rejects the city that he has served. In this action Coriolanus is the victim of his own foolish desire for consistency in all phases of human behavior. He demands perfection in himself and expects it of others, but when he does not get it, he rejects the faulty person. In short, he lacks tolerance and human understanding.

The scene ends with the aedile calling for cheers of rejoicing; the people oblige, praising the "noble tribunes," and the stage is left empty.

Summary: This scene in which Coriolanus is banished crowns the rising action of the play and is structurally an important turning point. This approach is quite common in Shakespearean tragedy, where the action almost invariably reaches a high pitch at the end of the third act, then falls slightly in the fourth act to finish strongly in the fifth with the death of the hero.

1. This scene shows the political maneuvering of the tribunes, Sicinius, and Brutus.

2. It demonstrates the foolishness of the crowd that can so soon be swayed from its adulation of Coriolanus as a military hero to its condemning him as a traitor and an object of hatred to be banished from Rome.

3. In terms of the political implications of the play this scene is a case history of the evils of government by the people. We must, however, remember that here this kind of government really means mob rule.

4. The intense dedication of Coriolanus to the pursuit of honor is shown. His anger really becomes uncontrollable only when his personal honor is attached. Then he cannot keep silent.

5. In his departure from Rome Coriolanus refuses to bow his head, despite his rage. In that way he has salvaged some self-respect, while the populace have come off rather badly, especially their leaders, Sicinius and Brutus. One is left with the nagging suspicion that in banishing Coriolanus, Rome has banished the wrong man, despite his faults.

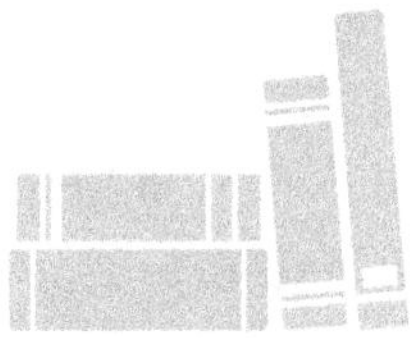

CORIOLANUS

TEXTUAL ANALYSIS

ACT IV

ACT IV: SCENE I

This act opens in Rome before a gate of the city. Coriolanus enters, accompanied by Volumnia, Virgilia, Menenius, Cominius, and members of the young nobility of Rome. All are sad and some are weeping. Coriolanus is the only one who seems remotely cheerful as he tells his followers to wipe their eyes. He gives the impression that he expects his banishment to be only brief, and again he refers to the Roman mob as "the beast/With many heads."

> **Comment: The image of the Lernean hydra destroyed by Hercules appears again. It is a fitting image for Coriolanus to use, since he sees himself as the savior of Rome and the performer of impossible tasks.**

Above all, Coriolanus seeks to console his mother, Volumnia. He tells her to take her own advice and remember that the worst situations are the occasions when a noble spirit best reveals itself. To behave like a gentleman when wounded requires a special knowledge. These are some of the precepts she had taught him.

Comment: This little episode gives us an unexpected insight into the education that Coriolanus had received from his mother. She has apparently been accustomed to teach virtue by means of maxims and proverbs. When Coriolanus runs out of such easy answers he is in a highly confused state of mind.

Virgilia weeps at her husband's attempts to cheer up everyone, and Marcius has begun to comfort her when Volumnia lashes out verbally against all the tradespeople of Rome. Coriolanus, however, seems to have more confidence than anyone else and claims that the populace will love him once they miss him. He compliments his mother on her strength, saying that she is capable of performing half the labors of Hercules.

Comment: Note the reference to Hercules again. This time too it is implicitly Coriolanus' own view of himself as a man of strength in battle.

And so Coriolanus says goodbye to the sorrowing Cominius and the weeping Menenius, begging Cominius to put some courage into the other members of the company. He promises his mother, too, that though he is leaving Rome without any companions, he is going like a lonely dragon into his marshy lair where he will be even more feared than when he is seen. He insists that he will still do better than the normal run of humanity, or else be destroyed. Volumnia begs her son to make specific plans before he leaves, and Cominius offers to go with him until he is settled in exile so that communication between him and his friends will not be broken. After all, if the possibility of his recall should arise, his friends would want to know where to find him. Caius Marcius refuses the kind offer of the aged general and asks his friends to escort him to the gate, saying that they will hear about him, and that he will always remain true both to himself and to his ideals. Then, alone, he leaves the city.

> **Comment: In the Plutarch source Coriolanus leaves Rome with a few friends, but nothing further is said of them. Here, Shakespeare's change obviously increases sympathy for the hero.**

SUMMARY

This scene serves the purpose of showing the nobility of Coriolanus in adversity, and indeed he is at his most likeable in this scene. He cheers up his companions and seems to retain a certain optimism that Rome will eventually need him again. One cannot of course say whether this attitude is supposed to be real or merely feigned in order to make his friends and relations less unhappy at his departure.

ACT IV: SCENE II

As Coriolanus and his supporters leave the stage, Sicinius and Brutus enter with an aedile and start discussing the departure of their enemy. Now that he has left Rome they arrange for the aedile to disperse the crowd. Between themselves they discuss the manner of their future behavior, now that they have achieved their purpose in getting rid of Caius Marcius. Sicinius notes that they have incurred the hostility of a considerable proportion of the nobility, and Brutus suggests that now they have shown their power they ought to lie low and seem most humble in order to ingratiate themselves again.

Comment: This brief exchange shows the tribunes as a pair of image-conscious political trimmers. They are more concerned with practical politics than the good of the city and wish to remain friendly with both sides. After all, their position and their power depend on their diplomacy.

Then, in this moment of their success, they catch sight of Menenius and the three ladies of Coriolanus' party, whom they naturally want to avoid, particularly Volumnia, who they say is mad. They are too late, and Volumnia utters imprecations on their heads, wishing that all the plagues of the gods be visited on them. Even Virgilia speaks up in this situation when she forces Sicinius to listen to Volumnia's speeches. Sicinius tries the technique of ironic insult, which has succeeded so well against the ever-touchy Coriolanus, but it is a poor weapon against Volumnia, who turns the tables on him, saying that he has craftily banished a man who has done more service to Rome than Sicinius has ever spoken words. Sicinius, thinking himself secure in his position as tribune, and seeing Volumnia as a mere distraught female, then asks Volumnia what would happen if she were to get her wish and Coriolanus were to confront him in the Arabian desert. But to our amazement and that of the tribunes, the answer comes from Virgilia and it is surprisingly bloodthirsty. Coriolanus would kill the two tribunes and destroy their posterity, a suggestion Volumnia promptly takes up.

Comment: Note the speeches of Virgilia here. They are short, but to the point, and show that she is certainly not a cowed creature. In fact she shows some of the strength and obstinacy we have already seen when she defied Volumnia in I.iii.

Sicinius and Brutus then engage in some of the most hypocritical conversation of the play when they piously wish that Coriolanus had continued to do Rome the same service he had done her in his earlier life. Volumnia in reply tells them that she knows who set the populace against her son, and says that they, the tribunes, are totally unfit to judge the great warrior. By this time even the hardened politicians are a trifle embarrassed and they leave, pursued by Volumnia's angry words. Then the four supporters of Coriolanus leave as well, Volumnia declaring that she nourishes herself on her anger.

Summary: This scene is designed to show different reaction to the banishment of Coriolanus.

1. The tribunes are self-satisfied and pleased with their underhand work, and they don't want to talk to the women.

2. Volumnia utters angry words and manages to frighten even the hardened politicians.

3. Even the gentle Virgilia is stung to make a savage retort to the men responsible for banishing her husband. In some respects her outburst indicates the sorrow of the two women even more than the imprecations of Volumnia which, after all, are expected.

ACT IV: SCENE III

This next scene, which takes place on a highway between Rome and Antium, gives another kind of reaction to the banishment of Coriolanus when a Roman and a Volscian meet. The Roman, Nicanor, is obviously part of the Volscian spy network, and the

Volscian, Adrian, has been sent to meet him. Nicanor tells of the strange insurrection of the Roman people against the patricians and the rulers. Adrian is surprised to hear that the riots are now over and says that the Volscians are in full warlike preparation to move against Rome now that she is distracted with internal troubles. Nicanor remarks that the conflict has continued to smoulder, even since the banishment of Coriolanus. The announcement totally amazes the Volscian, who tells Nicanor that this news will indeed be welcome to his masters. Nicanor agrees and says that Tullus Aufidius will now have an excellent chance to prove his mettle as a soldier since his great opponent will be out of the competition. The two spies depart merrily, happy in the knowledge that Rome is now vulnerable to an assault by the Volscian force.

Comment And Summary: This scene is primarily one of **exposition** and it gives the Volscian reaction to the banishment of Coriolanus. At the same time it also shows how vulnerable Rome is without her greatest warrior as her defense in time of peril.

ACT IV: SCENE IV

This scene is set in Antium. Coriolanus enters, poorly dressed and muffled as a disguise. He admires the city and remembers the havoc he has wrought in it by causing the deaths of many young men. Hiding his identity for obvious reasons, Coriolanus accosts the first citizen he sees and asks the way to the house of Tullus Aufidius, if he is in Antium. Left alone in front of Aufidius' house, Coriolanus meditates upon the fortunes of the world and of life in general which turn things so topsy-turvy that friends are found duplicitous and hostile while those formerly thought to be foes are now sought out as friends. Chance is indeed a strange thing, and Coriolanus finds that he now hates his birthplace and loves instead this enemy town. He makes up his mind to enter the house of Aufidius and take the risk that the Volscian general may slay him. Should this happen, it will be nothing more than he deserves in the way of justice, but should Aufidius give him the chance, then Caius Marcius can do the Volscians some service.

Comment And Summary: This very short scene, mainly taken up with Coriolanus' only soliloquy, is very important in establishing some of the motivations of the Roman, and it is about the only time we ever get close to what he thinks and feels. He does not joyfully turn himself into a traitor. Instead he sees himself as forced by circumstances into the situation of working for the opposing side. A man who fights for personal honor alone can really have no ties of country. His loyalty must remain due to an ideal of self.

ACT IV: SCENE V

The scene now shifts to the interior of the house of Aufidius where a banquet is in progress. Coriolanus enters and realizes that he certainly cannot pass as a guest, something that the two serving men make quite clear as they tell him brusquely to leave.

> **Comment: The behavior of Coriolanus is most notable here, because instead of playing the part of a poor stranger he immediately reacts as a noble person when an inferior tries to push him out of the way.**

Coriolanus tells the serving men to get out of the way and leave him alone, something that rather confuses them. The servants try politeness to get him to leave, but Coriolanus, with the arrogance of one accustomed to command, overcomes all objections. Intrigued by this odd stranger, the serving men question him, and when asked where he lives, Coriolanus replies that he dwells under the heavens, in the city of birds of prey, kites, and crows.

Comment: Coriolanus actually says "Under the canopy," a word which contains the double meaning of the heavens, and also the canopy borne by servants over the head of a monarch or a noble person walking in procession. This may indicate Coriolanus' desire for glory and greatness. Further, for Caius Marcius, Rome is indeed a city of birds of prey.

The serving men take up this last remark and ask if he dwells with jackdaws, foolish birds, as well. To this question Coriolanus replies that he does not serve Aufidius.

Comment: This remark does not mean that Coriolanus considers Aufidius a fool, but rather that those who serve him are foolish jackdaws.

After this display of bitter wit Coriolanus rather arrogantly beats one of the servants. In the meantime another serving man has gone to fetch Aufidius to order this importunate stranger out of his house. The general comes quickly and asks the muffled figure to identify himself. Coriolanus does not answer immediately, trying to see if Aufidius will recognize him, and giving him a hint that his name is unpleasant to Volscian ears, and harsh in Aufidius' own. Aufidius is still puzzled, but he notes both Coriolanus' grim appearance and the commanding air of his face, and is perceptive enough to note that beneath the threadbare clothing this stranger seems to be noble.

Comment: This delay on the part of Aufidius in recognizing his enemy is dramatically effective in terms of creating suspense, and it can also be realistically motivated. After all, Aufidius has been accustomed to seeing Coriolanus only in his war gear, with his face at least partially hidden under a helmet.

Coriolanus now takes off his scarf and reveals himself, telling Aufidius that the only thing he has left to him from his valorous days in Rome is the title Coriolanus, which is not of course a diplomatic one to use in Antium. Everything else has been taken from him by the cruelty of the Roman populace, and what is more, the nobles have permitted this to happen. They too have forsaken him and have allowed the voices of slaves to shout him out of Rome.

Comment: Note here that the rage of Coriolanus is now directed against all Rome, not merely the populace. After all, the nobles were also in some measure to blame because they took the easiest way out.

Caius Marcius then goes on to explain his motives in coming to the house of Aufidius. Certainly he doesn't fear death, otherwise he would hardly have come to the house of his deadliest enemy. No, his motives proceed from pure desire for vengeance on all those who banished him. In other words, Coriolanus has a proposition to make. He wants to work with Aufidius, and he will fight like an infernal spirit against his own people.

Comment: The proposition is not all one-sided. Coriolanus does have something to offer, but he needs an army to carry out his plan, and the only way he can raise one is to join that of Rome's enemy.

Here Coriolanus is thinking in terms of personal vengeance for his wounded honor. He is pursuing a peculiarly personal concept of honor, not patriotism, and it is this faulty attitude which lies at the root of many of his errors of behavior. Shakespeare almost alienates our sympathies from Coriolanus at this point of the play chiefly because he does not give any thoroughly detailed study of the ways by which Coriolanus reached his decision to defect.

Coriolanus concludes by saying that if Aufidius is not agreeable to the suggestion then he, Coriolanus, offers his unprotected throat to his enemy, telling Aufidius that he would be a fool not to take the opportunity. He almost dares him to slit his throat.

Comment: Ironically, in this speech to Tullus Aufidius, Coriolanus shows that when he wishes he is perfectly capable of civil discussion, something he did not show in Rome. Here, however, he is speaking to an equal whom he respects, not a crowd which he despises. The important thing is that these two proud warriors speak the same language of honor, so that Coriolanus does not have either to beg or to flatter.

Aufidius' reply is almost immediate and it shows a different side of his character from that of the disgruntled, hate-ridden, defeated warrior of Act I. Seeing his enemy in such an unfortunate situation brings out the natural generosity of Aufidius. He cannot forbear a noble action. If he cannot outdo Marcius by force of arms, then he will outdo him in generosity. He embraces his erstwhile enemy and claims that every word Caius Marcius has uttered has weeded another root of malice from his own heart. He greets the Roman in terms which recall the words of Caius Marcius himself in the first act. He felt no greater joy when his beloved wife first entered his house than he did in seeing Caius Marcius here in his house.

Comment: These two warriors actually do have something in common. They consider themselves wedded equally to war and to their wives. They use the metaphors of wedding and war interchangeably.

Aufidius then speaks of the immense Volscian army, and says that he had planned to do battle once more with Coriolanus.

Comment: Aufidius claims that Caius Marcius has beaten him twelve times, but in I.x he had said five times. Shakespeare is confused somewhere.

Fighting with Coriolanus seems to have become almost an obsession with Aufidius because he speaks of dreaming about doing battle with him. Even if the Volscians had no other quarrel with Rome than that the city had banished Coriolanus, Aufidius says that he would raise an army to avenge him. Joyfully he invites Coriolanus into the banquet chamber to meet the Volscian senators who have come to feast his departure. Incidentally, Aufidius says that his army had been made ready for attacks on Roman territories rather than on Rome itself.

As Coriolanus thanks Aufidius for his kind reception, the Volscian makes an astonishing gesture of generosity. He calls the Roman a most perfect man, treats him with respect, and offers him half of his own command. After all, the Volscian can make use of Caius Marcius' specialized knowledge of the strengths and weaknesses of the Roman territories and the city fortifications as well. The two warriors go into the banquet hall.

Comment: Aufidius' generosity is quite sincere at this point of the play. He is genuinely glad to see Coriolanus because he respects his nobility and military skill. After all, a man is measured by the stature of his enemy, and Aufidius is basically a man who cannot resist a generous and spontaneous action, though there is still a streak of smallmindedness in him. At this point of the action he is on top, but as he commences to lose reputation among his own men the envious side of his nature will be shown. Plutarch really did very little with the character of Aufidius until this point in his tale of Coriolanus.

So far everything seems to be going well for Caius Marcius, and now the serving men comment on the strange happenings they have just witnessed. They all congratulate themselves on not treating the unknown visitor too roughly, and now they all seem to remember something notable about him. Then they start to compare the relative military prowess and reputation of Coriolanus and Aufidius. The First Servingman even seems to claim Coriolanus as greater than Aufidius.

Comment: Shakespeare is here using his frequent practice of having a common character pass judgment on the greater ones of the play. Their unsophisticated remarks are apt to be honest, although the servants are a trifle guarded and deliberately confusing here. At the same time their comparisons point forward to what will happen to Coriolanus.

An even more important hint about coming events is given by the Third Servingman in calling Caius Marcius "he that was wont to thwack our general." Then a further debate ensues concerning the merits of the two warriors, the First Servingman supporting Aufidius and the Second Servingman, Coriolanus. The Third Servingman expresses his astonishment at seeing the Volscian senators bareheaded before Coriolanus, while Aufidius was hanging on his every word. Lastly, Aufidius has divided his power with Coriolanus and everyone at the table has approved.

Comment: This continual comparison of the virtue and valor of Coriolanus and Aufidius hints towards a dissolution of the alliance that has been made so quickly. Aufidius has been beaten by Coriolanus rather too frequently for his own self-confidence. In addition, by giving Coriolanus equal command, Aufidius is breaking one of the cardinal rules of government. He has done away with a strong central authority. Something is bound to go wrong when command is divided.

Apparently Coriolanus has said that he will destroy Rome. The serving men realize that war is about to begin and, unthinking, foolish men that they are, they rejoice in the fact. After all, peace is dull, and they look forward to the day when Romans are held as cheaply as Volscians. With a shout they opt for war as preferable to peace.

Summary: This scene is extremely important for the way in which it indicates the character and motivations of both Coriolanus and Aufidius.

1. Coriolanus is shown as enraged against the entire population of Rome, the plebeians for banishing him, and the patricians for permitting them to do so.

2. Coriolanus does not think of himself as a traitor, but rather as a man who must avenge a stain on his own

personal honor. Essentially this attitude is selfish, but Coriolanus cares more about his own personal consistency than public opinion and patriotism.

3. In the only notable soliloquy given to Coriolanus we learn a little about his motivation in going to the Volscians. An unspoken reason is of course that he needs an army for the pursuit of his vengeance, and here is one ready at hand.

4. In Antium Coriolanus must display political astuteness, and he shows much more political skill than he seemed to have in Rome. In Antium, however, he is talking to a warrior of equal rank who understands him.

5. The discussion among the serving men, comparing Aufidius and Coriolanus, points forward to what will happen in the next act when the Volscian is again competing with Coriolanus.

6. Aufidius is shown as a generous character who appreciates Coriolanus' worth. Nevertheless, there is still a hint of smallmindedness which cannot allow him to play second fiddle to a man whose military skill exceeds his own.

ACT IV: SCENE VI

The scene now returns to Rome, where Sicinius and Brutus are congratulating themselves on their actions in getting rid of Coriolanus. Sicinius comments that no one in Rome hears anything about him, and obviously any counter measures that his friends might take will have no effect on such a peaceful city. The people are now happy and quiet, where before they had been in turmoil.

Comment: This speech may also indicate that any counter measure Coriolanus might take would be bound to fail.

Sicinius claims that Coriolanus' friends are really rather embarrassed that everything is going so well in Rome, alleging that the patricians actually prefer to see the populace in a state of confusion instead of working peacefully in their shops. Brutus agrees with his fellow tribune and says that they took their stand at just the right time. At this moment Menenius enters and Sicinius remarks that he has grown very kind and tolerant lately. The tribunes greet him and Sicinius cannot forbear the gibe that Coriolanus is not missed much in Rome at large, only by his friends. Further, the Commonwealth is carrying on very peacefully; the rage of Coriolanus has absolutely no effect on it. Menenius replies moderately that things are going well, and would have gone better if Caius Marcius had been of a more compromising mind and tongue. And in reply to the tribunes' question he says that not even Coriolanus' wife and mother hear anything from him.

A few citizens then enter and greet the tribunes with respect, and the reaction of Sicinius and Brutus is almost royal in its paternal condescension. Brutus sanctimoniously wishes that Coriolanus had loved the common people as much as their tribunes had. The grateful citizens depart and the tribunes continue to preen themselves on their success, Sicinius saying how much better things are now than when "these fellows" (the crowd) were in rebellion. Brutus again returns to the subject of Coriolanus, saying that he was a good warrior, but insolent, self-centered, too proud, and too ambitious, while Sicinius adds the charge that he wanted to rule alone. Menenius, of course, disagrees, but the tribunes remain secure in their self-satisfaction.

Comment: This scene is built on ironic contrast. Everything the tribunes say must be seen against the background of the last scene in Antium. Note too how the tribunes treat the common people as inferiors. Once again, Brutus reveals himself in his misreading of the character of Coriolanus, because the warrior was not really ambitious for power, believing quite honestly that the rule of the many was unwise for Rome. Again, in his apparently selfish actions, Coriolanus was actually pursuing a limited ideal of personal honor, which he cannot compromise and continue to live with himself.

The contentment of the tribunes is suddenly dispelled with the entrance of an aedile bringing news that a captured slave claims that the Volscians with two separate armies have entered Roman territories to lay them waste. Menenius jumps to the conclusion that Aufidius must be emboldened by the news of Caius Marcius' banishment. The tribunes, however, react blindly and stupidly. Sicinius tells Menenius not to talk about Marcius, while Brutus gives orders that the rumor-mongering slave should be whipped. They are obviously disturbed, but ostrichlike they refuse to admit that the Volsces "dare" break peace with Rome; after all, that would show the defeat of their policies. Menenius, on the other hand, sees only too clearly the possibility of a Volscian attack; he has already seen three in his lifetime. Wisely, he recommends against whipping the slave, who might not then reveal the source of his information. After all, he may be telling the truth, and this may be a timely warning. The tribunes refuse to listen.

A messenger then arrives to say that all the nobles are congregating at the Senate and that they seem to expect bad news. Sicinius now orders the whipping of the slave only to be told that the rumor has been confirmed with an addition. Menenius then reveals what he has apparently known all along, that Caius Marcius is said to have joined with Aufidius to lead an army against Rome in order to inflict the ultimate vengeance on the city. The tribunes treat this news with contempt, Brutus saying that it is merely a trick to bring the vacillating citizens to wish Caius Marcius home again. Menenius optimistically tends to discount news of the alliance because of the great enmity between the two warriors. But then another messenger confirms that part of the rumor as well.

Cominius now enters and promptly begins to attack the tribunes, ironically telling them that they are really responsible for the ravishing of their own daughters and the coming destruction of the city, which he pessimistically sees as unavoidable. Then in answer to Menenius, Cominius says that Coriolanus is almost the god of the Volscians and leads them like a superhuman being. In turn, they follow him against "us brats" of Rome with the same confidence that children chase summer butterflies, and less thought than butchers give to killing flies.

Comment: The reference to children and butterflies is an ironic echo of I.iii where Young Marcius, the son of Coriolanus, chased a butterfly and in anger pulled it to pieces. Then this behavior was called "One on's father's moods," a statement which seems a fair comment on the current situation in Rome, whose destruction is a mere nothing to Coriolanus.

Menenius now turns on the tribunes and ironically congratulates them on the success of their work and that of the stinking, garlic-eating mob. Coriolanus will shake Rome down about their ears as Hercules shook down ripe fruit.

Comment: Menenius here refers to another of the labors of Hercules, the stealing of the golden apples of Hesperides. Again a comparison of Coriolanus with Hercules gives the former added stature.

Brutus, suddenly a trifle humbled, for the first time in the play uses an address of respect to a patrician in enquiring after the truth of the rumor. Cominius confirms it, saying, in addition, that the territories revolt happily against Rome and that resistance to the forces of Caius Marcius is considered valiant, but utterly foolish and hopeless.

Menenius remarks that Rome is lost unless "the noble man," Coriolanus, has mercy. Cominius asks who can possibly beg him for it, and indeed he is right. The tribunes cannot ask, because of their part in the banishment, and neither can the people, because their voices banished him. His friends are just as bad because they permitted the tribunes and the mob to have their own way, and therefore they are the equivalent of enemies. Menenius agrees and says he couldn't even plead with Caius Marcius to save his own house. Then, ever the rhetorician, he turns on the tribunes with a devastating remark:

...You have fair hands, You and your crafts! You have crafted fair (IV. vi. 118-119)

Comment: This refers to the tradesmen and artisans who called themselves the "hands" of the tribunes. They also are craftsmen, working with their hands. But crafts carries the additional meaning of the underhanded intrigue of the politicians, the tribunes who "crafted fair" to get Coriolanus out of their way.

The tribunes now show themselves wretched cowards who refuse to accept the responsibility for their actions. Menenius denies the guilt of the nobles for the current state of affairs, but admits their cowardice in permitting the mob their will, while Cominius shrewdly comments that he is afraid the fickle mob will "roar him in again." In other words, they will look out for their own self-interest, not the good of Rome. The only thing the city can do is fight against the alliance - and even Tullus Aufidius obeys Coriolanus.

A troop of citizens now enters, and Menenius castigates them for their part in exiling Coriolanus. Now he is coming back to exact reparation, and Rome deserves what is coming to her. The citizens try to shift the blame and say that many of them thought it was a pity that Coriolanus was banished, and after all, they only acted for the best, as they thought. Cominius taunts the mob as mere voices, "You and your cry," an ironic reminder of Coriolanus' farewell, "You common cry (pack) of curs." The patricians then leave for the Capitol, while Sicinius tries to control the situation by claiming that the patricians are trying to make political capital out of it. They really want this rumor to be true. The citizens leave, grumbling that they had never been fully committed to the idea of banishing Coriolanus. Left alone, the tribunes admit that they don't like the sound of the news and hope it is untrue.

Summary: This scene, built on ironic contrast with the preceding and succeeding scenes, is important for its expository function and its revelation of the attitude of Rome itself.

1. It shows the real attitude of the tribunes to be rather hypocritical and cowardly. They seem to treat their own people as inferiors.

2. The patricians are shown as accepting guilt for their part in banishing Coriolanus. They should not have given in to the mob. Note that they do not seem to consider Coriolanus a traitor; they think his action quite justified in view of the treatment he had received from his native city.

3. The citizens are cowardly and fickle. They try to shift the blame to minimize their part in the coming disaster.

4. Coriolanus the warrior strikes more fear to Rome than Coriolanus the politician. No one doubts his inflexibility of purpose and everyone seems convinced that no appeal to mercy will sway him from his intended course. His vengeance is considered just. Ironically, the despised Volscians now seem to think more of Coriolanus than did the Romans for whom he shed his blood.

ACT IV: SCENE VII

The scene now shifts to the Volscian camp, just outside Rome, where Aufidius is speaking with his lieutenant and asking whether his troops still fly to follow Coriolanus. The lieutenant says that he doesn't quite understand the "witchcraft" or superhuman power of the Roman, but his soldiers treat him as a god, invoking him as the grace before meals and speaking constantly of him. In this expedition Aufidius' own valor is denigrated, even among his supporters. In reply Aufidius says that he doesn't want to disturb things at the moment while the expedition is going on, but he is disturbed by the proud bearing of Coriolanus, even to himself. But as he says, one cannot expect a man of Caius Marcius' nature to behave differently.

Comment: Shakespeare has altered Plutarch here to give Aufidius better motivation for his later hostility to Coriolanus. In the source the Volscian forces had been divided into two parts. The first, under Coriolanus, was detailed to do the actual harrying of outlying Roman settlements, gradually subduing them in the march toward Rome. The second, under Aufidius, was basically engaged in garrison duty. Naturally, the soldiers under Coriolanus had more chance to obtain booty and that is the major reason Plutarch gives for their desertion of Aufidius.

The lieutenant wishes that Aufidius had either run the whole expedition himself, or else left it solely to Coriolanus. The mistake was to invite comparison. Aufidius sees the point, but hints that he will find something to accuse Coriolanus of, when he must give an accounting of his policy and behavior toward Rome. At the moment he is doing good service for the Volscian state and is fighting like a dragon. Sooner or later Aufidius will have the chance to destroy him. The lieutenant then asks his general if he expects Coriolanus to capture Rome, and Aufidius says that he has no doubt of his success. His personality is magnetic, the nobles and governors of Rome are his supporters, the tribunes have no military ability, and the populace will recall him just as hastily as they banished him. He will devour Rome as an osprey, a fish-hawk, devours a fish.

Aufidius then recapitulates Coriolanus' career, commenting that he served Rome well, but could not carry his honors with suitable humility. He wonders about the reason. Was it personal pride arising from too frequent success, was it faulty judgment in failing to seize opportunities, or was it inability to be other than the warrior trying to rule peace and war in the same way?

Certainly one, or all, of these possibilities made Coriolanus feared, hated, and finally brought about his exile.

Comment: This speech shows Aufidius a very astute critic of human nature. He sums up the major motivations for us, but does not attempt to answer the questions which Shakespeare here has him recapitulate for expository purposes. The two warriors have an almost occult understanding of each other, much more so than the politicians. In addition, the fact that this reasoned assessment comes from an enemy lends it more weight.

Aufidius then shows himself appreciative of the merits of Coriolanus, which almost outweigh his faults, but then in a few proverbs he indicates his intention to drive out his opposing fire, Coriolanus. The concluding couplet of the scene states his future policy more directly: he will attack Coriolanus after he has captured Rome.

Summary: This scene reveals the characters of Aufidius and Coriolanus and points forward suspensefully to the conclusion of the play.

1. Coriolanus is apparently acting as arrogantly as ever. His personality is consistent, but it rubs Aufidius the wrong way.

2. Aufidius is jealous of Coriolanus because his own men flee to the banner of his rival. Thus he is conscious of his inferiority.

3. Aufidius gives a reasoned assessment of the motives, faults, and virtues of Coriolanus. This shows the

astuteness, and in some measure the nobility, of Aufidius, and gives a rather unbiased opinion of the hero.

4. Aufidius hints that he will destroy Coriolanus, but he will bide his time and wait until Rome is captured. He will not jeopardize the success of the expedition. Aufidius is here a much shrewder politician than Coriolanus.

CORIOLANUS

TEXTUAL ANALYSIS

ACT V

ACT V: SCENE I

This last act opens in a public place in Rome. Menenius and Cominius, together with Sicinius, Brutus, and other Romans, come in. Menenius says that he will not go to plead Rome's cause with Coriolanus since the warrior has refused to talk to Cominius, the general. Certainly he has been very close to Coriolanus, but that won't help. He suggests that the tribunes and those who banished him go to the Volscian camp to kneel as petitioners before Coriolanus. He himself will just stay at home. Cominius seems almost heartsick that Caius Marcius would not even deign to recognize him, though once he did say his name. At that point Cominius had urged the claims of old acquaintance and fellowship in arms, but Caius Marcius would not even answer to the proud name of Coriolanus. In fact he forbade all names for him, saying that he was a nameless nothing until he had made a reputation by burning Rome.

Comment: This incident indicates how deeply Caius Marcius has been hurt by Rome's rejection of him. He also sees that he must make a totally new reputation in terms of valor, and he wants no part of honors given by a city that has banished him. Now he must make a new life in service to another country in order to retrieve his lost personal honor.

Menenius again upbraids the tribunes as Cominius tells of the unsuccessful arguments he used in an attempt to soften the resolve of Coriolanus. He suggested that granting pardon when it was least expected was a noble, a royal act, but Coriolanus refused to grant his petition from a state that had punished him as a subject. Cominius then suggested that surely Coriolanus did not wish to destroy his friends, but Coriolanus replied that he didn't have the time to sort out a few good grains from a heap of smelly chaff. This last remark touches Menenius to the quick; he himself is one of those few grains, as also are Virgilia, Volumnia, Valeria, and Young Marcius. They must all be destroyed for the sake of the majority.

Comment: Shakespeare is most economical here in having Cominius recount the course of his interview with Coriolanus. It would be undramatic to portray separately this petition scene and the two that are to follow, and further, this one is the least important to the action, though the cumulative effect of them helps to soften Coriolanus' heart. The three petitions are arranged in an ascending order of emotional emphasis and a gradual decrease in reasoned argument, beginning with a companion in arms, followed by a close friend who is almost a father, and culminating in a plea from Caius Marcius' own family.

Sicinius still begs Menenius to try his luck with Coriolanus and says that he is the person most likely to get Coriolanus' ear because of his close relationship to him. Brutus adds his appeal to that of his fellow tribune.

Comment: The tribunes here seem to be implicitly admitting that Rome's only chance for salvation lies with its naturally and divinely ordained leaders, the patricians.

At this point Menenius agrees to go, and he really thinks that he has a chance of success. Incurably optimistic to the last, he suggests that possibly Coriolanus needed a good meal when he sent Cominius away. He is much more likely to accede to a request after a good dinner.

Comment: Like so many other people in this play, Menenius makes the mistake of judging Coriolanus by the standards of normal, lesser men. In so doing he reveals his own pleasantly epicurean and everlastingly optimistic disposition. Note the way in which the tribunes are now paying compliments to the patrician. They are indeed skilled in working with other people.

Cominius, however, remains pessimistic; he saw Coriolanus enthroned with his eye as red with rage as though it would burn Rome with its own heat. The banished man had simply bidden him rise and dismissed him without another word. His conditions for surrender he sent by letter, but said that he was bound by oath to the Volscian cause. As far as Cominius sees things, Rome's only hope is to send Volumnia and Virgilia to see him, and they apparently do intend to go.

Comment And Summary: This scene shows the depth of the pessimism that pervades Rome and contrasts it with the hardness of purpose that Coriolanus shows in seeking vengeance on the city. Cominius, rejected himself, thinks that Menenius will also fail. He believes that an appeal from the women of Coriolanus' family is Rome's only chance.

ACT V: SCENE II

This scene takes place in the Volscian camp before Rome. Menenius arrives, and is challenged by the watchmen. He states his business and identifies himself as "an officer of state" come to speak with Coriolanus. When refused admission he gives his name, confidently expecting it to be recognized and insists on seeing the young general. He tells the watchmen of his admiration for Coriolanus, and even orders them to let him pass, but of course the guards tell him to return to Rome. Nothing seems to put Menenius off, and finally the watchmen start baiting the old man with tales of what they will do to Rome, and when that does not work, they threaten him with physical violence. Even then Menenius persists.

At this moment Coriolanus and Aufidius enter, and significantly Coriolanus speaks first, asking the watchmen what is the matter.

Comment: This is one of the little things that indicates how impossible it is for Coriolanus to remain under anyone's command. One wonders who is really the superior officer here, Coriolanus or Aufidius.

Menenius seizes the opportunity, and with a combined gibe and threat to the watchmen, he throws himself at the feet of his "son" Coriolanus, wishing for his prosperity, and offering his own tears as water to quench the fire that Coriolanus is preparing for Rome. He begs Coriolanus to pardon Rome and assuage his wrath on the watchmen, if necessary. Coriolanus, however, simply tells him to go, and in answer to Menenius' question, he says he knows no ties of affection, not even to the members of his own family. His personal power to pardon Rome now resides in the hearts of the Volscians, whose cause he has espoused. He tells Menenius to forget their past friendship rather than poison it by his present ingratitude. Nevertheless, since he did once love Menenius, he gives him a letter to take back to Rome, but he refuses to listen to his pleas.

As Menenius prepares to leave, Coriolanus turns to Aufidius, almost as if asking for congratulations on his singlemindedness, and says that the old man had been one of his most beloved friends in Rome. Aufidius replies dryly that Coriolanus is indeed steadfast in his purpose. Left alone with the watchmen, Menenius is taunted by them and he leaves brokenhearted, with barely enough strength to insult them. The watchmen express admiration for the strength of "our general," Coriolanus, who, like a rock or an oak, will not be shaken by the wind of Roman petitions.

Comment And Summary: This scene, with its extended baiting of Menenius, is in part an interlude before the arrival of the Roman women, but it is also used to create suspense. Coriolanus has now denied all affection, including the ties of family. This statement prepares for the next scene and also indicates the excessive consistency of Coriolanus.

ACT V: SCENE III

This scene takes place within the tent of Coriolanus, where he is busy arranging last details of battle strategy with Aufidius.

Again one wonders who is really commanding the army, since Coriolanus refers to Aufidius as "my partner in this action," and then tells him that he must report to the Volscian lords telling them how well he, Coriolanus, has performed in the action.

Comment: For a man who objected to the peremptory shall of the tribunes, Coriolanus is very careless in his own use of the imperative. This incident simply indicates his air of command at all times. He is insensitive to the feelings of others, especially when he is pursuing a single course of action.

Aufidius offers testimony to the loyalty of Coriolanus, saying that he has shut his ears to the pleading of Rome, and has held no private conversations with Romans, not even his friends. Warming to the subject, Coriolanus tells what it meant for him to send away beloved old Menenius, who had almost made a god of him. Obviously, by sending him, the Romans indicate their desperation. Once again Coriolanus has offered Rome the same peace conditions which they had already refused. The only reason he offered them once more was to soften the blow of his refusal to the old man. From now on, he declares, he will not listen to any private suits from Rome, no matter who comes. This remark is punctuated by a shout outside, but Coriolanus declares that he will not break his vow.

Virgilia, Volumnia, Valeria, and Young Marcius, with attendants, now come into the tent. Coriolanus is a trifle taken aback, but he speedily fights down the affection that wells up in his heart, and also any feelings of duty that he may have. Then, as he looks on them, his resolution begins to melt, and he muses aloud that for his mother to bow to him is as if Olympus, the abode of the gods, should bow to a molehill. Even Young Marcius seems to beg his father not to deny him. But this weakness is a passing one, and he says that he will never be such a young goose as to obey his affectionate instincts. No, he will stand firm as though he were self-begotten and had no family.

Then Virgilia speaks to him as "My lord and husband!" and Coriolanus melts with affection for her. He greets her with sadness for her sorrowful face, and realizes that he has forgotten the part he has set himself to play. He begs her to forgive his tyranny, but tells her not to ask forgiveness for Rome. Oblivious of everything else he kisses her passionately, and then realizes that he has forgotten to greet his mother, so he turns and kneels before her.

Volumnia tells him to stand, and then she kneels before him in supplication, deliberately reversing the roles of child and parent. This is too much for Coriolanus, who raises her. For a mother to kneel before the child she has chastised is a total violation of the natural order of things. When such an occurrence comes to pass, order is destroyed in the universe and impossible things happen: pebbles snap their fingers at the stars, and winds strike the cedars against the sun.

Comment: This kind of image which shows the results of the flouting of authority is very common in Shakespeare.

Volumnia greets Coriolanus as the warrior she has helped to make and introduces Valeria to him. Respectfully he speaks to the beautiful and chaste maiden.

Comment: This little troop of suppliants is well chosen to attack Coriolanus at his most vulnerable emotional points. Apart from their physical relationship to Coriolanus, the three women

represent the three states of a woman's life, chaste maiden, wife, and mother-widow. Each pleads in her own person for a different group of Roman citizens, while young Marcius appeals to Coriolanus' sense of honor and reputation in posterity.

Coriolanus greets his son fondly and wishes that he may prove invulnerable to shame and that his thoughts may always be noble. At Volumnia's order the child kneels before him. But Coriolanus cuts his mother short and says he doesn't want to listen to any petitions because he has already made up his mind to deny mercy to Rome. He won't dismiss his troops and he won't treat with the Roman multitude; he doesn't want to be told that he is unnatural, and he doesn't want anyone to try to assuage his wrath.

Comment: In this speech Coriolanus indicates that he is rather shaken by the appearance of those whom he loves. Consequently he tries to anticipate their arguments so that he will avoid the emotional turmoil of having to listen and then deny them. This sensitive side of Coriolanus appears but rarely in the play.

Volumnia, on hearing these terms, says that they have come to ask precisely what he has just denied, but nevertheless, they will speak so that their failure, if they fail, will be laid at the door of Coriolanus rather than blamed on their own inefficient pleading. Trapped, Coriolanus asks Aufidius and the assembled Volscians to remain and listen, because he wants to have no private conversations with Rome.

Following up her advantage, Volumnia tells Coriolanus to look at the shabby dress of his family and to ask what their lives have been like since his banishment. Their misfortunes are such that the very sight of him makes them weep rather than rejoice. From this emotional plea she moves skillfully to one combined with patriotism, asking him to think how it must be for them to see him, a son, a husband, and a father, destroying his country. And how can they pray for their country's welfare when their loyalty is divided? If they pray for their country, then they are in effect praying for the death of the man they love most, and to whom they owe their first loyalty. If they pray for him, they must lose their country. In either case he will be ruined: he will either be led as a foreign criminal through the streets of his native city, or else will be congratulated for destroying both his city and his family. She then offers him defiance. If she has anything to say, he will march on Rome only over her body, over the womb that bore him, something that she will not permit. And Virgilia adds her defiance to Volumnia's. Marcius also defies him - just like a younger edition of his father. He'll run away until he's old enough to fight back.

Comment: By bidding Coriolanus to think of the aftermath of his attack on Rome, something he has not thought of before, Volumnia is using a very powerful argument. Coriolanus is really caught in a dilemma, though he does not admit the fact. He has never been able to see more than one course of action at a time, and therefore anything that clouds the issue seems to confuse him. Probably for the first time in his life he is in a situation in which any decision will be partly right and partly wrong. His upbringing, which seems to have simplified all issues into conflicts of right and wrong, has not prepared him for such an eventuality, and he doesn't know quite what to do.

Volumnia, however, presses her advantage. She is not asking her son to save Rome by destroying the Volsces. That would run counter to his personal honor. She is merely asking him to use his influence to reconcile the opposing forces so that the Volsces may take pride in the mercy they have shown, while the Romans will be both humbled and grateful for the mercy they have received. Then he will be praised for his part in arranging this peace. After appealing to his pride in achievement, she returns to the matter of personal honor and reputation, saying that if he allows Rome to be destroyed, posterity will say that his last act wiped out all the nobility of his former valor and service. His name will be forever accursed. She asks whether it is noble to hold a grudge, and calls upon Virgilia and Marcius to speak in her support, but they remain silent, Virgilia in tears.

Then Volumnia tries another approach, one not shown elsewhere in the play. She begs Coriolanus to remember the love she has shown to him and appeals to his filial affection, upbraiding him because he has never in his life shown her any special consideration, although he has been her only son, to whom she has given up her entire life. Let him spurn her and deny her request; she is simply doing her duty as a mother. This thrust strikes home, and Coriolanus turns away. Quickly Volumnia falls to her knees and bids the other suppliants do likewise.

But since that seems to have no effect, Volumnia plays her last card, one that she has used before - contempt. Coriolanus is so proud of his valiant title that he has no pity left. Very well, they will go back to Rome and die. She tries to use Young Marcius, saying that the child argues the rightness of their petition more than Coriolanus has strength to refuse. Then she throws out her last insult; Coriolanus, "this fellow," had a Volscian for his mother, he is married in Corioli, and Young Marcius is like him only by accident. She then asks leave to depart. She will remain silent until the city is burning, and then only will she speak.

Comment: This is a most eloquent and skillful plea in which Volumnia tries almost every possible approach, including an emotional appeal. In many ways her most important attack is that of contempt, and in the suggestion that he is really a Volscian, all the contempt of a proud Roman matron for a lesser tribe is shown. When she says "his wife is in Corioles" she probably has two meanings in mind. After all, Coriolanus has spoken of being wedded to war, and in a sense war is now his sole wife. Since he is now allied, or wedded, to the Volsces, his wife (war) is figuratively in Corioles.

It is this last, disdainful attack which finally breaks Coriolanus. Since contempt succeeded with him before, in III.ii, when he refused to plead in the market place, some critics have argued that Coriolanus is actually afraid of his mother. When she rounds on him with insults he thus becomes a whipped urchin once again, almost blubbering for approval. This suggestion seems to be an overstatement. Coriolanus does not fear his mother's chastisement of him, but in using insult Volumnia is using a weapon he understands because he uses it so often himself. Here he is vulnerable to attack from his own weapon because Volumnia has softened him up by pleas for his love and affection. And of course Shakespeare could not make his great military hero little more than a child scared of a whipping. Coriolanus has, of course, always sought her approval, because she is the source of all his knowledge of honor and valor. This is the reason that her contempt is so hard to bear.

At the end of the speech Coriolanus "holds her by the hand, silent," according to a stage direction that sounds like Shakespeare's own. Then he speaks, claiming that the gods must be laughing at this unnatural scene of a mother pleading with her son. He congratulates her on having won a happy victory for Rome, but he foresees that it will be fatal for him. The course she has set him on can only lead to his death. But with a sudden shift, Coriolanus is again the soldier. Death is inevitable, and so he turns to Aufidius and says that though he cannot make good wars, at least he can make a suitable peace. Then, almost as if asking for support, he asks Aufidius if he would not have done the same thing, to which Aufidius replies grudgingly, "I was moved withal." Now that he has made a decision Coriolanus is almost jovial, and remarks that it is no small thing to make him weep. He asks Aufidius to decide the terms that he, Coriolanus, should make with Rome. Then he sends his family and Valeria back to Rome, saying that he will not return with them, but asking their support in the whole business.

Comment: In this scene Coriolanus has discovered mercy, but he has also learned another lesson: that his total dedication to the cause of his own personal honor has been a very limited vision indeed. On some occasions revenge for personal injury must give way to a higher cause - duty to country and family. By the end of this interview with Volumnia, Coriolanus has thus become a much larger-minded character than he was at the beginning of the play. He must now reconcile this decision with the situation in which he finds himself with the Volscians. He has said that he will offer peace, and therefore he is bound in honor to do so, but at the same time he must fulfill his commitment to Aufidius. Therefore he must remain in Antium. Incidentally, Coriolanus does not consult with Aufidius at all when

he capitulates to Volumnia. He simply takes it for granted that the decision is his to make.

Aufidius in an aside hints at what will happen and also sums up the nature of Coriolanus' dilemma. Mercy and honor are now opposed within his rival so that out of this conflict and the resultant decision. Aufidius will be able to restore his own power.

Coriolanus finally dismisses the women and says that they deserve to have a temple built in their honor. No one else in all Italy could have arranged this peace.

Comment: This occurrence was supposed to be the reason for the building of the Roman Temple of Women's Fortune.

Summary: It is impossible to overestimate the importance of this scene which is climactic in the play.

1. It puts Coriolanus in a new light, showing his love for his family.

2. It shows a basic weakness in his character, an inability to decide when two courses both contain elements of right. Finally his natural nobility brings him to choose mercy.

3. Coriolanus learns that mercy is not weakness, and also, through the discovery of affection, he learns a larger concept of honor and patriotism than he had known before.

4. Volumnia is shown at her very best and is one of Shakespeare's greatest mature female characters. She is the embodiment of a staunch Roman matron in every way.

5. Aufidius is given the evidence he needs to destroy his rival.

6. Coriolanus gives Aufidius cause for jealousy, and in his attachment to personal honor he voluntarily puts himself in Aufidius' power, though knowing the outcome will be death.

7. Coriolanus must return to Antium to justify himself to the Volscians.

ACT V: SCENE IV-V

The scene now turns to a public place in Rome, where the pessimistic Menenius speaks as though the ladies' mission to Coriolanus is a hopeless gesture. Caius Marcius has grown from a man to a dragon.

Comment: Menenius is the third person to refer to Coriolanus in these terms: Coriolanus himself and Aufidius are the others.

Sicinius objects that Coriolanus had always loved his mother dearly, but Menenius says that will be irrelevant. Coriolanus is nothing more than a hard, tough, efficient fighting machine, totally without mercy. Sicinius utters a brief prayer to the gods, but Menenius says that he doesn't expect help from that quarter, since in banishing Coriolanus Rome had no thought of the gods.

A messenger then bursts in, telling Sicinius to flee immediately because the plebeians have offered violence to Brutus, swearing that they will kill him by inches if the Roman women are not successful.

Comment: Again we have evidence of the unpredictable and fickle nature of the mob. Coriolanus was right about the way they change sides impulsively. The Roman citizens en masse come off very badly in this play.

The first messenger is immediately followed by another announcing that the ladies have been successful, the Volscians have retired, and Caius Marcius has left. Immediately rejoicing breaks out and music sounds. Menenius sets off to meet the women, saying that Volumnia is worth the entire city, including such tribunes as Brutus and Sicinius, who is lucky to have saved his wretched neck. Sicinius offers thanks to the messenger and all withdraw.

Straight away a procession of senators and lords enters, bringing with it the Roman women. The senators call for cheers. Another senator then calls for a shout of welcome to Coriolanus' mother to repeal the sentence of banishment on her son.

Comment and Summary: Scene iv shows that Coriolanus has been right about the fickle and unpredictable nature of the mob. Anyone can use them, but they will just as quickly turn on those they have formerly followed. Scene v is, of course, meant to show the joy of Rome at her deliverance, but it also shows the changeable quality of the mob, which now thinks to undo by a shout of welcome the damage done by a shout of banishment. There is irony in congratulating Volumnia on a victory which will destroy her son.

ACT V: SCENE VI

This scene returns to Antium, where Tullus Aufidius enters with some attendants.

Comment: Some editors have substituted Corioles for Antium here, but Plutarch is quite specific in making the last actions of Coriolanus' life take place in Antium.

Aufidius sends a package by his attendants to the lords of the city of Antium. Obviously it is a letter of accusation against Coriolanus' and Aufidius says that he will vouch for its truth in public. Coriolanus, in the meantime, has entered the city gates and intends to absolve himself of blame with words.

Three or four conspirators who support Aufidius now enter, and a guarded conversation takes place. One of the conspirators offers to deliver Aufidius from the danger they had formerly discussed, if he still has the same purpose. Aufidius says they will have to wait until they see the behavior of the people, and the conspirator remarks that the people will always remain uncertain while there's a difference of opinion about the two (Coriolanus' name is not mentioned, but it is obviously implied), but the fall of either one will leave the other in sole command. Aufidius then proceeds to a recital of his own grievances, claiming that he has endured enough to justify his hostility. After all, he raised Caius Marcius to be a commander in the Volscian army, and pledged his own honor for his trustworthiness, only to have his protégé flatter his way into new friendships. Again, the vaguest language is used: "He watered his new plants with dews of flattery." He alienated Aufidius' friends from him, and even bent his previously unbowed head for that purpose. The conspirator recalls that Coriolanus had been notably stiffnecked in Rome.

Comment: If Aufidius is telling the truth, then Coriolanus has learned the lesson of soft talk for purposes of expediency.

Aufidius goes on to detail the ways in which he befriended Coriolanus, making him equal with himself, giving him his own way in everything, even allowing him to choose the best men from his own troop, and in return his men seem to have considered the glory of the expedition to be solely that of Coriolanus. Finally, Aufidius has been repaid by arrogant treatment, for Coriolanus has chosen to patronize where he should have given respect. The First Conspirator says that the entire army has wondered at Aufidius' patience. But the last straw for Aufidius was the way in which he sold a perfect chance to sack Rome for the tears of a few women. Aufidius therefore vows that Coriolanus shall die, and he will regain his own lost power with the fall of his enemy.

Comment: Aufidius does seem to have some reason to be jealous of Coriolanus, but the charge he really intends to use is his failure to take Rome with its rich spoil.

The conspirators feed Aufidius' anger by telling him of the jubilant reception Coriolanus has received from the people while Aufidius, their legitimate leader, entered his own town unnoticed. The Second Conspirator speaks of the stupidity of the crowd, who shout for the man who caused such slaughter among their children. The Third Conspirator therefore advises Aufidius to seize the advantage before Coriolanus has the chance to open his mouth to move the people with speech. Then, since the only version known will be that of Aufidius, anything in favor of Coriolanus will be buried with him.

The lords of the city enter at that point to welcome Aufidius, at the same time regretting to hear the charges that he has written against Coriolanus. The earlier faults might have been punished with small fines, but the unpardonable offence was to give up just where he should have begun (with Rome, in other words), not returning by way of spoil the expenses of the expedition. Making a treaty where he could have made a victory is not to be condoned.

Coriolanus now enters with drum and flags, followed by the people. He tries to put a good face on things, saying that he has returned a loyal soldier of the Volscians, still uninfected by love of country. He speaks of leading an army to the very gates of Rome and says that he has managed to defray one third of the expedition's expenses with captured booty. Then he offers the argument that the peace with Rome brings as much honor to the people of Antium as humiliation to the Romans, and with a flourish produces the agreement, signed and sealed by the Roman authorities.

Comment: Shakespeare never makes it quite clear whether Aufidius actually had a hand in drawing up the peace terms. Certainly Coriolanus did ask him to decide in V.iii, but it is also possible that Caius Marcius took the responsibility on himself. Aufidius, on the other hand, may not want to admit his part in the negotiations.

Aufidius then calls on the lords, telling them not to read the agreement, but instead to tell the traitor that he has abused the powers granted to him. Coriolanus immediately picks on the word traitor and asks what is meant. Aufidius makes the application quite specific with "Ay, traitor, Marcius." Coriolanus picks up the name Marcius questioningly, and Aufidius asks if he expects to hear his "stol'n name / Coriolanus in Corioles."

Comment: These lines give critics the idea that this scene is laid in Corioles. Probably Shakespeare was either careless or unable to resist the sound of the lines.

Aufidius then flings the principal charge at Coriolanus: he has traitorously betrayed the cause and given up the city of Rome for a few tears from his wife and his mother. He makes great emotional play with the words "your city" of Rome, impressing the fact on the Volscians that the city was so nearly theirs. Enraged, Caius Marcius invokes Mars, but Aufidius tells him not to call on the god of war, "Thou boy of tears."

This insult from the slightly older man infuriates Coriolanus, as Aufidius had intended, and so he sallies forth to attack the Volscian with words, calling him a slave, and claiming in the vernacular of the duel that he will give him, "this cur," the lie. He impugns the courage and military prowess of Aufidius and recalls his own military superiority to him. One of the lords tries to get in a word, but Coriolanus is now in full cry and shouts defiance at the entire assemblage of Volscians, daring them to cut him to pieces. He repeats Aufidius' insult of "boy," and calls him in reply a "false hound," taunting him and the company with his own superlative exploits right inside their own town of Corioles.

Comment: Coriolanus is always vulnerable to insult, something that Aufidius knows very well. Therefore he has laid this very successful trap, which is an ironic echo of the banishment scene in Rome (III.iii). Coriolanus cannot control his hot temper and here, where he might have been able to turn matters to his own advantage, he fails to make use of his new self-knowledge and throws away his chances by indulging in contemptuous insult.

Aufidius makes the most of the situation, claiming that Coriolanus had merely been lucky in Corioles, and anyway, why should the Volscians listen to such a braggart who tries to shame them. The conspirators call for his death, and the expectedly fickle multitude join in the cry, now remembering the slaughter that Caius Marcius had wrought on the Volscian forces in earlier wars. But even here there is a man of moderation, a lord who calls for peace, saying that Coriolanus is a noble man and justly famous throughout the entire earth. He deserves a fair trial, and therefore the lord orders Aufidius to stand firm and not trouble the peace. Coriolanus, however, is in a blind rage after his military prowess has been insulted, and he offers to fight six Aufidiuses at once. This last insult gives Aufidius his chance, and all the conspirators call "Kill." They draw and kill Caius Marcius who falls to the ground dead. Aufidius stands on his corpse to use it as a platform in defense of his action.

Comment: Shakespeare here alienates the sympathy of the audience from Aufidius because he is treading contemptuously on a man whose conduct has shown him to be much greater than the Volscian. The lords speedily remind him of his place in this regard.

The lords are horrified at what has happened and tell Aufidius not to tread on Coriolanus. Aufidius is quite surprised at the hostility the killing has caused and finds himself forced to justify his action. He claims that Coriolanus was a danger to the state, and offers to defend his conduct before the Senate, or else endure the censure of the lords.

The First Lord then orders that the body of Coriolanus be removed and decrees that the city will mourn for him as the noblest corpse that ever a herald followed to his burial urn.

Comment: These words allude to the custom of having a herald follow the corpse of a noble or valiant man, proclaiming his rank and noble deeds to the populace.

In extenuation of Aufidius' conduct, another lord draws attention to Coriolanus' own impatience and insulting anger, contributing factors which ought to lift some of the blame from Aufidius.

Then Aufidius pronounces what is in effect an **epic** funeral oration over the body of the hero, his former enemy. He says he is "struck with sorrow," and we should probably believe him. He then asks three of the highest ranking soldiers to take up the body and bear it from the place with the sound of the drum and with the trailing pike customary for the funeral of a great soldier. Despite the slaughter that Coriolanus caused among the young men of the Volsces, he will nevertheless be given a noble memory.

> **Comment: This last speech, though spoken by the man who plotted the death of Coriolanus, is not hypocritical. It is an honest expression of sorrow for the death of a noble and honorable opponent. The end of the play shows us once again the generous side of Aufidius, who undertakes an action of respect automatically. Incidentally, any expression of admiration from an enemy is doubly impressive as a conclusion to the play. Note, by the way, that it does not seem to have been the weapon of Aufidius that struck down Coriolanus, but rather one belonging to one of the conspirators, a fact which emphasizes the irony of Coriolanus' life and death.**

Summary: This scene rehearses the ultimate downfall and the ironic death of Caius Marcius Coriolanus.

1. It shows the plotting of Aufidius against Coriolanus and attempts to explain the reasons for his enmity.

2. The people of Antium are shown to be just as fickle as those of Rome. At first they admire Coriolanus, but are soon turned against him.

3. Aufidius accuses Caius Marcius of being a traitor, an ironic echo of the scene in Rome (III.iii), and uses as his major argument his failure to take Rome and thereby gain booty for the coffers of the Volscians.

4. Coriolanus at first has the crowd with him, but he remains vulnerable to insult and becomes enraged, instead of attempting to talk his way out of the situation, something Aufidius fears. Through his rage Coriolanus forces a fight that ends in his rather ignominious death.

5. Despite the accusations of treachery, the Volscians as a whole and Aufidius in particular, finally recognize the true nobility of Coriolanus. They give him a funeral worthy of his rank and military prowess.

6. In his last speech Audifius pays tribute to his fallen enemy in the **epic** manner. Here he is being quite honest, for Coriolanus was a deeply flawed, yet a very great man, and the manner of his death seems undeserved.

Conclusion: More than any other tragedy of Shakespeare, Coriolanus leaves one with a great sense of waste. Throughout the play Coriolanus is shown as a man of infinite possibilities and potentialities, none of which he really fulfills. Finally, he comes to a death which cannot in the remotest degree be termed heroic, for he is slain in an undignified brawl over some rather stupid insults. Yet at the same time his death is consistent with his life, because he has always lost his temper whenever his touchy personal honor is attacked. His chief trouble is that he is totally unable to compromise, and lacks the greatest gift of all - moderation. Only once does he show this virtue, when he spares Rome, and then his act is destructive to him. His ability to translate his rage into action makes him a superb soldier, but his inability to control his temper makes him a misfit in time of peace. In short, he is a man of tremendous virtues, and fatal faults, almost inextricably mixed.

The play also raises a great many important questions about the nature of personal and political government, as well as the nature of honor, but it does not answer any of them. If anything, we must infer that the play approves an aristocratic system of centralized government as best for a state, and that government by the many is something to be avoided. These are not comforting words today in a democratic age. Nevertheless, when one looks at the "wheeler dealer" machinations of the tribunes, Sicinius and Brutus, a disconcerting suspicion remains that neither politicians nor human nature have changed. Shakespeare offers no simple solution in this extremely sinewy and intellectual play; we are forced to make up our own minds about the characters and the occurrences. The characters are in their essence all too human and complex, and the occurrences all too typical and familiar to us in the twentieth century. Here we have an interesting case in Coriolanus, because the play has steadily become more and more relevant to our own day.

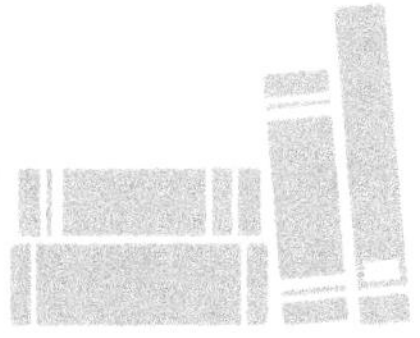

CORIOLANUS

CHARACTER ANALYSES

Coriolanus

Coriolanus is, of course, the reason for the existence of the play. He is the most important character and the mainspring of all the events, both good and evil. All other characters are in effect foils to him, showing up various aspects of his character, or reacting against him. Coriolanus possesses an abrasive personality, but there must almost always be qualifications in any attitude held towards him. Even when he is acting in a manner which naturally calls forth our hostility, we find ourselves forced to see a germ of truth in his argument, or considerable reason behind his action or his attitude. At the same time no other Shakespearean tragic hero is given so many virtues and so many unlikeable traits. In fact, Shakespeare risks alienating the sympathies of his audience.

Coriolanus has immense personal pride, and in that respect the tribunes assess him correctly, but his pride is based on something normally considered a virtue: a noble concept of personal honor. The trouble with his attitude toward honor is that it is limited to the personal. He strives for total consistency in his own behavior and expects it from others. His mother has taught him a strict and unyielding code of action, with the result that he despises anyone who cannot live up to the ideal that he himself not only professes but also follows. On all occasions Coriolanus considers the impact of an action upon what today we might describe as his own self-image. If it then seems dishonorable, he refuses to follow that path.

So far this notion of honor seems totally admirable, but it contains the seeds of its own destruction. By continually following a code impossibly staunch for anyone else, Coriolanus has become incapable of respecting anyone who compromises for any purpose whatever. Personal honor has become a way of life, and a selfish one, excluding all other personal relationships and considerations of even larger scope, such as patriotism or loyalty to a cause.

Even in his most notable achievement, Coriolanus shows himself more than normally proud. He is the greatest soldier of Rome and he delights in killing. In some ways he is Rome's most efficient war machine, and he is totally lacking in any sense of fear. He is ruthless in his attacks, and after his achievement within the walls of Corioli he dashes forth in search of battle in other parts of the field. War for him is life itself, and as G. Wilson Knight comments, Coriolanus is at his best as an instrument of destruction.

All the foregoing sounds highly patriotic, but what are the real motives behind Coriolanus' great valor? At the beginning of the play one of the citizens claims that "he did it to please his mother and to be partly proud, which he is, even to the altitude of his virtue." In some respects this assessment is correct. Caius Marcius is absolutely secure in his own valor, which he considers a mere act of duty. The motive behind the duty is not so much patriotism, but personal honor. And since Coriolanus does not know the meaning of fear he is totally contemptuous of normal mortals who do. Consequently he shouts imprecations at his soldiers when they break ranks and flee before superior odds; unemotional himself, he cannot understand the feelings of others. This is another symptom of his limited vision of personal honor.

This narrowness is shown again when the army tries to reward him for his valor. He hates to hear himself praised, and it would be pleasant to say that he is modestly and genuinely embarrassed in the face of praise. Unfortunately, such is not the case. Coriolanus is too proud to understand that he has done anything worthy of note. He has simply done his duty, and since he is naturally better in battle than most men, more is expected of him. No praise is due for the performance of duty; therefore he cannot accept it. But there is also another aspect of pride involved; by accepting the adulation of the army he is also accepting the praise of lesser men, those whose valor he despises. By however much he does so, by that amount is his glory lessened. Therefore in his pride he quite brusquely refuses the proffered tenth of the army's spoil, and instead accepts two things which are rather typical of the man: a good war horse as a gift from Cominius, whom he respects, and the honorific title of Coriolanus, in memory of his personal triumph. Anything more tangible might give the impression that his sword was being paid for and that his motives were pecuniary. Also, he cannot accept gifts from men he despises.

This contempt for men of lesser rank and virtue is shown early in the first act. The citizens speak of his hostility to the common people, and indeed he is "a very dog to the commonalty." He sees the people as lacking the commonest forms of decency, with stinking breaths and cowardly minds. Here the aristocratic ideal of virtue is paramount, and he thinks that the aristocrats, being naturally superior to the plebeians, have a divinely-ordained duty to govern lesser people. Consequently, his rage when he hears that the plebeians have been granted five tribunes as political representatives is understandable. He sees this move as a wanton overturning of the established order of authority, and a weakening of centralized authority.

Such a superior attitude is one thing in war, where perhaps some kind of hardness is required, but it is wrong in a political situation. It is Coriolanus' inability to translate himself from war to peace that contributes to his downfall. As a soldier he is magnificent, but he cannot frame himself to the realities of practical politics, and he tries to bring this rigid and unbending code of military honor into the world of social and political compromise. His pride will not permit him to ask gladly and humbly for the voice of people he despises, and therefore he seems to mock the people. At first they give their voices, but then by changing their minds they give Coriolanus evidence that his attitude toward the fickle mob is right and that compromise with them is wrong. Then one of the greatest shocks he receives in the play comes when Volumnia begs him to flatter the people. She argues expediently that the end sometimes justifies the means. Coriolanus cannot fully agree.

His pride is shown even more notably in his banishment from Rome. Coriolanus must on all occasions have the initiative against lesser people, and therefore he cannot accept the mob's sentence of banishment on himself. He must himself banish the ungrateful mob, otherwise by accepting sentence he would be taking himself at their evaluation. Coriolanus is always susceptible to insult too, and Sicinius manipulates him brilliantly by flinging a charge of treason at him, as Aufidius also does at the end of the play.

Motivation for Coriolanus' treatment of Rome after his departure can also be blamed on his faulty concept of honor and its consequent pride. His honor has been impugned in his banishment, and therefore he must take personal revenge. He does not believe that he is acting as a traitor. Shakespeare is here less kind to his hero than Plutarch, his source, who sees the alliance with the Volscians as a kind of political alliance of the Roman patricians and the Volscian nobles against the plebeians. In Shakespeare the conflict is more personal: Coriolanus wants vengeance on the entire population of Rome. Incidentally, no one in Rome seems to consider Coriolanus' desire for vengeance as anything other than justified in view of his shabby treatment by Rome. The major difficulty with the character of Coriolanus is really that Shakespeare has drawn him from the outside, and has given him only one sizeable soliloquy to display his motivations (IV.ii). Thus we never really get to know him, and since he is almost always totally sure of himself, we have no human conflict with which we can identify.

The only time that Coriolanus demonstrates any conflict within himself comes in the pleading scene with his wife and mother. Here he rises to perform a single act that goes beyond his concept of personal honor, and at that moment he achieves true greatness in a spiritual sense. At this instant of enlightenment he sees that he has lived by an inadequate code. But the result is ironic, because in discovering that he can act according to the emotions he has also ruined himself. He has nowhere to go. He cannot return to Rome as a former traitor, and similarly he has violated the trust of the Volscians and cannot go to live among them. The only thing he can do to salvage any kind of honor is to return to Antium to give an account of his stewardship, and face whatever fate is in store for him.

Once more we find **irony** in his choice. Coriolanus knows he is going to his death, but the manner of it is not of his own choosing. He still rises to insult, and his ticklish personal pride still makes him treat the assembled crowd with contempt.

Finally he is killed, not by a noble warrior, but by a plotting conspirator, a lesser man, and Aufidius stands upon his lifeless corpse. But even then, and despite the fact that in some ways she actively sought his death, his nobility is what is remembered. Foolish and wrongheaded he certainly was, yet he was always honest and true to his ideals, faulty though they were. His ignominious death somehow seems undeserved, and his tragedy consists in the waste of a tremendous potential for good.

Volumnia

Second only to Coriolanus in importance is the character of Volumnia, his mother. She is unusual in Shakespeare because she is a mature woman, and since boys played female roles in the Elizabethan theater such parts were rare indeed. However, careful attention to the dynamics of the character shows that the masculine attributes that Shakespeare assigns to Volumnia make the part easier for a boy to play.

Volumnia is somewhere between fifty and sixty years of age and has long been a widow. Coriolanus is her only child and she has devoted her life to him and has largely made him what he is. She herself is the practitioner of all the traditional Roman virtues of staunchness, courage, austerity in behavior, patriotism, and devotion to honor. She sent Caius Marcius to battle against the Tarquins when he was about sixteen and rejoiced when he distinguished himself in that engagement. She is dedicated to the warrior ideal of ancient Rome and has striven to make her son the epitome of all the Roman virtues.

In many ways she has succeeded: she has reared a superb warrior totally devoted to the active pursuit of honor. But in her determination to avoid making her son a woman's man Volumnia has failed to teach him respect for other human beings. He has been taught none of the softer feelings, and though he shows love for his wife, he is contemptuous of lesser beings. Volumnia, with a certain amount of expedient political wisdom, can see where one should compromise, but her son cannot understand such an attitude, which seems to run counter to honesty.

The relationship between mother and son is an unusually close though perfectly natural attachment between two people who have meant everything to each other and who respect each other as well. Throughout his life Caius Marcius has tried to satisfy his mother's opinion and live up to the ideals she has taught him. In this respect the citizen who claimed that his brave actions were performed to please his mother was quite correct. Only when he comes home wounded, or in some other way manages to fulfill her ambition, does Volumnia grant him her approval. But in working so hard to avoid making a milksop out of Coriolanus, Volumnia has erred in the opposite direction. She has insisted so strongly on his matchless skill and superiority that he lives by a code which glorifies personal achievement for its own sake. Plutarch blames some of Coriolanus' shortcomings on the limitations of his education, but Shakespeare does not openly criticize the upbringing of his hero, and indeed it has been excellent in its way. Instead he builds up the relationship between mother and son and emphasizes the influence that Volumnia always exercises over Coriolanus.

Nowhere is this influence better shown that on the two occasions on which Coriolanus gives in to his mother's demands. The first comes in III.ii when Volumnia, in pursuance of her political ambitions for him, asks him to humble himself to the people. This apparent about-face is almost incomprehensible to Coriolanus, who holds out against all kinds of arguments except one: his mother's contempt and apparent total rejection of him. At that point he attempts, though unsuccessfully, to fulfill her wishes. Contempt is Volumnia's ultimate weapon against Coriolanus, and she uses it again in V.iii, when she pleads most eloquently for him to spare Rome. Here she makes a great concession in humbling herself before her son, something she has never before done. She has done a startling act in inverting the normal order of authority, but the cause is just - the salvation of Rome. Thus she shows herself to be larger-souled than Coriolanus because she can see beyond the limits of personal vengeance and, as before, she is infinitely more expedient and politic, as well as more skillful in argument. Nevertheless, she exhausts the arguments of personal affection and of patriotism without receiving any answer from her son. It is not until she openly defies him and turns on him with scorn that he relents.

This ultimate weapon of Volumnia is not merely one of chastisement for her son; it is her method of speaking his language. Only a proud spirit can communicate with that proud spirit, and only on that level can the two fully communicate. Coriolanus cannot bear to lose his mother's good opinion, but he is no whipped urchin and no immature oaf. He is instead respectful of the code of ethics to which they both subscribe, and his mother's contempt means that he has been unfaithful to the ideal. Her contempt is therefore almost unbearable in its revelation of his shortcomings.

Ironically, Volumnia knows that in saving Rome she is destroying the life of her son, but not without reason is she considered the staunchest Roman matron of them all. She sees her duty here as being towards Rome, not her son, and she follows the path that she sees as the only right one. And finally she is hailed as a heroine in Rome, as indeed she is, because she embodies in her behavior all the virtues for which Rome was popularly supposed to stand.

Virgilia

The contrast between Volumnia, the mother, and Virgilia, the wife of Coriolanus, is almost astonishing. Whereas the one is articulate and masculine, the other is the epitome of love, domesticity, and femininity. She has a mere twenty lines throughout the play, but rarely has Shakespeare so well suggested a character with such economy of means. Coriolanus once calls her "my gracious silence," and his affection is obvious in the few scenes they have together, but they are never actually alone. Virgilia is the embodiment of the Roman domestic virtues as Volumnia is the female embodiment of the public virtues. Virgilia sews, remains at home, worries about her husband's safety in battle, frets at the thought of wounds and blood, and brings up her young son.

She fears the military hardness of her husband, and when Volumnia and Valeria rejoice in the attributes that Young Marcius has received from his father, Virgilia hopes he will grow out of them. But she is not a negative character, despite her silences, and displays unexpected reserves of strength, and even of obstinacy. In our first meeting with her, she crosses wills with Volumnia, and wins-she remains at home while the other ladies go out. Virgilia is awaiting news of her husband and she does not want to be absent in case it comes. Her affection for Coriolanus is boundless, and her presence and tears in Act V do a great deal toward showing Coriolanus that he cannot deny the existence of emotion within himself, no matter how much he may wish to do so.

Valeria

She is the last of the female characters in this play and is very lightly drawn. In Plutarch, it is she who makes the suggestion that the ladies plead Rome's cause with Coriolanus. In Shakespeare she is given less to do, and in I.iii she is used chiefly as a foil for the development of Virgilia and the revelation of the character of Young Marcius. She represents the third important class of Roman womanhood - the chaste maiden. The three women thus represent the three estates of feminine existence, and as a result their pleas are stronger than might at first be expected. Valeria is a merry, beautiful, virtuous, and sociable person, and therefore her sorrow and silence on the mission to Coriolanus make a great impression upon him.

Young Marcius

He is an engaging child of about eight years who is given only a few lines to say, in V.iii, where he says defiantly that he won't let his father tread on him. He'll run away until he's old enough to fight. The incident of the butterfly, recounted in I.iii, shows that he has his father's quick temper and that his anger is quickly translated into violent action when he thinks himself injured, even if he has merely fallen down in pursuit of a butterfly. He is also used dramatically to arouse the emotions of Coriolanus in the pleading scene of V.iii.

Menenius

He is the most important patrician of the play and represents a very specific point of view. He is a thorough aristocrat, yet the plebeians consider him their friend, chiefly because he does not give himself airs and does not openly abuse the people. Nevertheless, he is a conservative, and he always seems to believe in supporting the status quo of settled government.

Menenius is given the most important statement on government in the course of the play, the famous anecdote of the belly and the members, in which he proves that the belly, representing the senate of Rome, ought to control the mutinous members, the citizens. What he states here is good, solid, conservative political theory, which seems to have been generally accepted in Shakespeare's day by orthodox political thinkers. The aristocrats, according to him, have a divinely-ordained right to rule, and the people ought to recognize that fact. Nevertheless, the nobles also have a duty to rule justly, and the people have a right to expect impartial justice. In short, all groups in the state have a place, and concomitant rights and duties. But the more one looks at this anecdote the more one sees that Menenius is really engaging in rather specious argument. He is assuming the truth of what he is trying to prove, and on several occasions he actually insults members of the plebeian class. They accept his comments, where they rebel against those of Coriolanus, because of the manner of their delivery.

In other words, Menenius has a sense of humor and does not stand on ceremony. He can make jokes about himself, and claim in a spirit of apparent camaraderie that he is a "humorous patrician" and "one that loves a cup of hot wine with not a drop of allaying Tiber in't;...one that converses more with the buttock of the night than with the forehead of the morning." In this way he can forestall with a laugh and a light comment the anger of those whom he is attacking. He believes in moderation in terms of action and continually tries to make peace between the warring factions of Rome. But these attempts at reconciliation when affections are inflamed are naturally quite fruitless.

What is often overlooked about Menenius is that he is a born politician with that easy air of authority which belongs only to a man who is completely sure of his own ordained place as a superior member of society. Such a man does not have to flatter openly; he can make jokes at his own expense, but he has such innate distance that none of the citizens, not even the tribunes, dare go too far with him. Later, when Rome is seeking for an emissary to Coriolanus, Menenius is the obvious choice because he has been extremely close to the young warrior. In fact he seems to have been involved in his education.

The old patrician, however, is not the shrewdest judge of character in the play, and like many people, he tends to rate others by himself. He is almost pathetic in his assurance that Coriolanus will be tractable after a good meal. His own epicurean taste is speaking there and not his knowledge of Coriolanus. Menenius is almost totally Shakespeare's own creation from a name and a single anecdote in Plutarch. What Shakespeare has done is to give him life and movement, and to use him dramatically as the nearest approach to comic relief in a notably austere play. He is also about the only character who weathers the storm of the play's action unscathed. As a man with little original thought he survives where his betters fail.

Tullus Aufidius

He is the real foil character to Coriolanus in terms of valor and political acumen. He is apparently a bit older than Coriolanus and is given a greater share of the action in Shakespeare than in Plutarch. He seems a somewhat contradictory character. Certainly he is noble, and at the same time he is generous with praise when he thinks it warranted; yet, like Coriolanus, he too is proud and he cannot brook a rival. He respects Coriolanus' military skill and thinks the young Roman the only person who is a worthy opponent for himself. However, after being defeated for the fifth time, he vows all kinds of vengeance, including the dishonorable one that would violate the relationship between guest and host.

Nevertheless, he has generosity, and we can take his openhearted greeting to Coriolanus in Antium quite seriously. Certainly Plutarch leaves no room for doubting his sincerity, because he does not show us the earlier threatened and angry Aufidius, simply the noble warrior greeting his rival. But what would seem to be Aufidius' motivation in both Shakespeare and Plutarch? In the first place there is no better way to discomfit an enemy than by offering him help when he is down. Further, killing a disgraced Coriolanus would not redound to Aufidius' own personal credit, because a warrior gains honor from the honor of his opponent. Again, Aufidius is a politic person and he knows quite well that a Coriolanus enraged against Rome will be a military asset to the Volsces, especially with his professional knowledge of the Roman fortifications. Finally, Aufidius gains great honor for his generous action. While this may not have been a conscious motive, we have seen that Aufidius is the kind of character who cannot refuse such a chance.

Shakespeare in Act I has also hinted at the major fault of Aufidius-his inability to put up with a rival, and gradually in the fourth and fifth acts we are shown the growing grievances of Aufidius. After all, Aufidius has a right to be angry, because Coriolanus does not ever really express gratitude in his words or actions; he becomes more and more arrogant, while the

Volscians begin to forget Aufidius and turn to Coriolanus. As a result of the invidious comparisons, the meaner side of Aufidius comes to the fore and he starts to plot against his rival. But unlike Coriolanus, he is shrewd and wishes to be sure that his actions can be publicly justified before he takes any open action against him. He is patient and will wait.

Finally, Aufidius understands Coriolanus better than the Roman knows himself. He knows how to taunt an enraged Coriolanus so that the blame for his death in the undignified scuffle does not fall fully on the instigator, himself. His standing on the corpse of his rival is a brilliant piece of functional stagecraft because it tends to anger us, the audience, who see Aufidius as the lesser man. Finally, Aufidius, the successful but now rather remorseful rival, is given the task of the **epic** funeral oration which is meant to be taken seriously as an honest expression of admiration. In some ways the character of Aufidius is contradictory and badly flawed, because Shakespeare in his dramatic economy does not give us all aspects of his motivation. Consequently, the combined meanness and generosity in his usually noble character do not always add up to a coherent whole. Nevertheless, he is a worthy foil to Coriolanus.

The Tribunes

Sicinius Veleutus and Junius Brutus are best treated together because there is not a great deal that differentiates them. They are both plebeians and the elected representatives of their class. What we must ask ourselves throughout the entire play is whether or not the tribunes are honest. Are they merely trying to hold on to the power deriving from their office for their own personal gain, or are they honestly working for the good of the city? Shakespeare leaves the answers ambiguous, and whatever opinion we ourselves hold is more likely to show our own personal bias than reasoned argument. If, however, we try to look at the tribunes in terms of the orthodox political thought of Shakespeare's day I think we must distrust the tribunes. After all, their first announced motive for opposing Coriolanus as candidate for consul is that "our office may,/ During his power go to sleep." This statement sounds more like fear of losing personal power than fear of losing a legitimate kind of grievance machinery. And again, in Menenius' biased opinion, the tribunes are not good dispensers of justice.

What the tribunes are particularly good at is political maneuvering, and here they can give lessons to most later politicians and organizers. They know how to manipulate a crowd and how to manage "spontaneous" responses to questions by distributing "yes-men" throughout the mob to lead the shouts. They put the idea of revoking their voices into the minds of some of the citizens and then skillfully offer to take the blame for their previous approval. But having set these matters in train, they hasten to the Capitol in order to hide their hand in the business. They can talk out of both sides of their mouths, agreeing with the patricians at one moment and using the crowd to banish Coriolanus the next.

In general each tribune supports the other, but Sicinius has a larger part in managing Coriolanus' banishment scene. There he shows himself expert in the understanding of character, inciting Coriolanus to anger, and then turning his remarks against him. In the meantime, Brutus keeps them also on the good side of the patricians as far as possible. One wonders, too, whether the tribunes do love the members of their class when we hear their comments about the people they use so shrewdly. Certainly, after the banishment of Coriolanus, the tribunes seem to act almost royally toward the people who had given them power.

Above all, the tribunes represent the principles of practical power politics, and they show only too well the dangers of the organized mass mind. By the last act, with Coriolanus almost at the gates of Rome, the tribunes seem to be cowardly, particularly when the mob, which they have manipulated before, turns against them. Finally, in their insistence that Menenius should intercede with Coriolanus, we have an ultimate **irony**: those who have stood for the will of the people now tacitly accept the role of the aristocrats as the ultimate saviors and guardians of Rome. In a moment of great danger all groups work together for the common good - Rome's salvation.

The Mob

Because of Shakespeare's insistence on the smell of the mob, and the way in which they are easily manipulated, many critics have concluded that the low opinion of the citizens often expressed in this play is, in fact, Shakespeare's own. There is absolutely no evidence to support such a conclusion, though one must admit that Shakespeare is kinder to individual members of the citizenry and servant class than he is to the rabble as a whole.

Here we should note that there are frequent interchanges of opinion among citizens concerning their rulers and betters and, in Act IV, among the servants who compare Coriolanus with Aufidius. On these occasions the comments of the individual, unsophisticated, ordinary people are more full of common sense and truth than those of their so-called superiors. Further, some of the grievances of the common people are absolutely justified, as Shakespeare makes quite plain.

What the play shows repeatedly is the horror that can result when the mass mind is influenced and controlled by demagogues and politicians. Then the mob is shown to be fickle and totally untrustworthy, looking out only for its current self-interest and on all occasions taking the short view of events. There is little to distinguish between the mob that banishes Coriolanus from Rome and the mob in Antium that calls for his death after having just greeted him with triumph. This fact would seem to indicate that while the individual members of the crowd may be trustworthy and wise, the collective mind is not.

Cominius

He is one of the minor characters of the play and is Consul at the time of the expedition against Corioli. As an older soldier with experience, he is in command of the Roman forces, and he seems to be a good general; certainly Coriolanus respects him. His treatment of his troops contrasts with that of Caius Marcius in that he is less bitter to them when they are forced to retire. He is extremely impressed with the valor of his young subordinate and wishes to reward him with a large part of the army's spoil. Failing in that attempt, he shows himself a shrewd judge of the young man by suggesting the only two gifts he will accept: Cominius' own war horse and the title Coriolanus. The general seems to have been fighting side by side with Coriolanus from the time of his earliest military expeditions against the forces of the Tarquins. He tries desperately to praise the deeds of the young man both before the army and later before the Senate, when Coriolanus is proposed for the office of Consul.

As Consul himself, he has considerable political power in the Senate and he is one of those who counsels moderation in Coriolanus' behavior. He is very close to the young man and even accompanies him to the gates of Rome, generously offering to go away with him. Towards the end of the play we hear that

Cominius has been to plead Rome's cause with Coriolanus, but has been sent back unheard. He is an honest man, a good soldier, an admirer of valor, and a true patriot. He disappears from the play after this rejection and we hear no more about him. His chief function is to act as a foil to the character of Coriolanus and to show the true, mature Roman ideal of valor and patriotism.

Titus Lartius

He is also an older soldier, and apparently he is even crippled, because he speaks of throwing away a crutch to fight the Volscians at Corioli. He is a general and second in command to Cominius. Coriolanus is his immediate subordinate at Corioli. Titus Lartius is not a fully-drawn character. Apparently he is an administrator, because he is given the task of settling affairs in Corioli. He, too, admires the valor of Coriolanus and attempts to praise him. Like Cominius, he seems to have power in the Senate and backs up his general's comments. Shakespeare uses him to convey messages of Aufidius' admiration, and hatred, to Coriolanus. He disappears after the third act, presumably for administrative garrison duty.

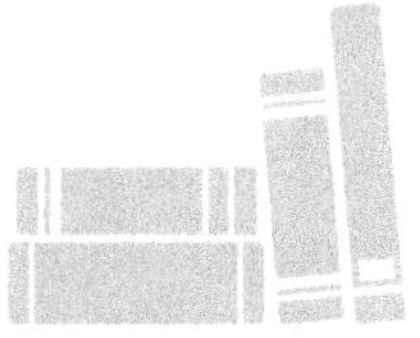

CORIOLANUS

CRITICAL COMMENTARY

GENERAL

The criticism of *Coriolanus* does not bulk as large as that of Shakespeare's other tragedies, and we must search for much of the commentary in works on the Roman and Greek plays rather than in studies of the tragedies. Further, criticism has been slow to look in detail at the Roman plays in general.

Certainly we have a few comments in the eighteenth century. Dr. Johnson refers in his *Preface to Shakespeare* (1765) to Thomas Rymer's complaint that Shakespeare did not make his Romans Roman enough, and John Dennis in 1712 said that Shakespeare did not distribute justice properly in *Coriolanus*, and objected to Menenius playing the buffoon. Johnson in the notes to his edition makes the surprising observation that *Coriolanus* is "one of the most amusing of our author's performances," but then his reasoning becomes clearer when we realize that he is actually praising the variety of action and characterization.

The nineteenth-century critics tended in general to follow their prevailing interest in character studies, though William

Hazlitt in 1817 maintained that *Coriolanus* showed such a tremendous knowledge of politics that it superseded most political treatises. In 1898 the Danish critic, Georg Brandes, published his two-volume *William Shakespeare*, in which he treated *Coriolanus* at some length (an unusual departure), seeing the importance of politics in the play, but also tying it up with the death of Shakespeare's mother. Edward Dowden, however, in his frequently reprinted Shakespeare. *A Critical Study of His Mind and Art*, placed the emphasis on the character of Coriolanus rather than on the political attitudes. This division of criticism still remains an important one.

However, for all its effectiveness on the stage, *Coriolanus* has not been as popular as it should be. Certainly critics like A. C. Swinburne and T. S. Eliot have been ardent supporters of it, but E. K. Chambers in *Shakespeare: A Survey*, seems to consider it a bit of a failure, "the exhaustion of a mood." D. A. Traversi does not agree, and neither does Mark Van Doren, though he notes that the character of Coriolanus is one with whom we have difficulty in identifying. In a brief mention in *Shakespearean Tragedy* (1904), A. C. Bradley sees in *Coriolanus* the beginning of the reconciliation **theme** which pervades the last plays, but in his *British Academy Shakespeare Lecture* (reprinted in *A Miscellany*), he seems less sure of this stand. And finally, for one of the best general studies of *Coriolanus*, from an actor-producer's point of view, we should turn to that of Harley Granville Barker in his *Prefaces to Shakespeare, Vol. II* (1947).

SOURCES AND TEXT

Two obvious places for a discussion of the text are E. K. Chambers, *William Shakespeare: A Study of Facts and Problems* (1930), and J. Dover Wilson's introduction to the New Shakespeare edition of *Coriolanus* (1960). For an excellent short treatment of Shakespeare's use of his major source, Plutarch, one should look at the introduction by R. H. Case to the Arden edition of the play, and particularly at a very detailed study of the same source by M. W. MacCallum in *Shakespeare's Roman Plays and Their Background* (1910). Suggestions that Shakespeare was also indebted to other important sources, such as Aristotle, Bacon, and other works of Plutarch, have been made by Fred Chappell, F. N. Lees, and Kenneth Muir.

IMAGERY AND POETRY

Imagery is usually treated within the context of general studies such as those of Caroline Spurgeon, Wolfgang Clemen, and Donald Stauffer, though A. C. Bradley in his British Academy Shakespeare Lecture makes an interesting case for the importance of fire **imagery**. The important common element in any discussion of **imagery** is the emphasis on its intellectuality rather than sensuality, as well as on such dominant images as those of the human body and various disreputable animals. J. C. Maxwell, in his article "Animal **Imagery** in *Coriolanus*" (1947), concentrates on this latter aspect. One of the latest studies of **imagery** is that of Maurice Charney (1961), which confines itself to the Roman plays and notes the many images of food and eating in this particular play.

Studies of the poetry are likewise to be found in larger works, and some of the more important include the remarks of B. Ifor Evans in *The Language of Shakespeare's Plays* (1951), while Mark Van Doren notes the rhetorical structure of the play. Paul Jorgensen, in *Redeeming Shakespeare's Words* (1962), makes some interesting observations on the use of the words "noble" and "nobility," particularly as applied to *Coriolanus*. In the same year (1962), G. Thomas Tanselle and Florence W. Dunbar also studied "Legal Language in *Coriolanus*."

BACKGROUND AND TOPICAL REFERENCES

Two useful accounts of Shakespeare's knowledge and treatment of Roman history are to be found in T. J. B. Spencer, "Shakespeare and the Elizabethan Romans" (1957), and J. Leeds Barroll, 'Shakespeare and Roman History" (1958). Frequently this topic is very closely linked to the political **themes** of the play and topical references. One of the most important studies in this regard is James E. Phillips, *The State in Shakespeare's Greek and Roman Plays* (1940). He believes that Shakespeare is making deliberate use of the Greek and Roman plays to teach political lessons to his countrymen. Whereas in the history plays Shakespeare treated problems which had precedents in English history, in the Greek and Roman plays he was more concerned with political problems which were relevant to England, but for which no English parallel existed.

Other topical references thought to exist in *Coriolanus* are often concerned with equations of the plays action with events in England, where the traditional conception of the state was being challenged and centralized rule was disappearing. E. C. Pettet parallels the riots of the play with the Midlands Insurrection of 1607, as also does Sidney Shanker, while W. Gordon Zeeveld, in "*Coriolanus* and Jacobean Politics" (1962), also sees the play as concerned with contemporary politics. And again, Paul Jorgensen offers some illuminating comments on the problems of the Elizabethan soldier in "Shakespeare's *Coriolanus*: An Elizabethan Soldier" (1949), and later in *Shakespeare's Military World* (1956).

POLITICAL THEMES

Most of the critical comment on *Coriolanus* seems to center on the political **themes** and the theories of government set forth in the play. Here James E. Phillips' work is of major importance, because he studies the **themes** against a background of Elizabethan and Jacobean political theory. As he notes the critics of the play fall into three groups: Stopford Brooke (1905) thinks that Shakespeare's sympathy lies with the people; Coleridge sees the playwright as objective; and the majority of critics believe that he shows contempt for the masses (p. 9). One of the best accounts of Shakespeare's treatment of the common people is that of Brents Stirling, *The Populace in Shakespeare* (1949). He shows that Shakespeare often shows pity for the weak and old, and uses individual members of the servant class for "whimsical, pertinent, and often intelligent commentary" (p. 57). Nevertheless, the mass, the mob, are treated badly because they have dared to go beyond their station and meddle in political affairs.

Other critics have continued to look closely at the political themes, and in 1936 J. W. Draper in "Political **Themes** in Shakespeare's Later Plays" saw a pattern of Renaissance preference for absolutism in government. He believed that these plays also showed the inefficiency of government in general. Anselm Schlosser in "Reflections upon Shakespeare's *Coriolanus*" (1963) saw this same conflict between aristocratic absolutism and "bourgeois demands," and while approaching the problem from a different psychological angle, Gordon Ross Smith noted "Authoritarian Patterns In Shakespeare's *Coriolanus*" (1959). Matthew Proser sees *Coriolanus* as really the symbol of Rome's disunity (1963), and L. C. Knights draws attention to the "personalism" of both *Julius Caesar* and *Coriolanus* in "Shakespeare's Political Wisdom ..." (1953). And, approaching the problem from a knowledge of military history, Paul Jorgensen discusses "Divided Command in Shakespeare" (1955), something that orthodox political thinkers of Shakespeare's day disliked.

In addition to studies of the aristocratic view of government, we have Kenneth Muir's 1954 article "In Defense of the Tribunes," and John Palmer's comments in *Political Characters of Shakespeare* (1945). Both these critics try to redress the balance in favor of the tribunes, and Palmer goes so far as to claim that they are acting from disinterested motives, considering only the good of the country. He thinks they honestly believe that *Coriolanus* would be bad for the country and therefore they resort not to dishonesty, but to the standard trickery of politicians, to gain their ends.

CHARACTERS

Just about everything written on *Coriolanus* has included material on political themes, and also on character, so that it is often difficult to separate the two. Of course the most important character is *Coriolanus*, who is analyzed under just about every heading in the critical commentary. A good general study is that of Harley Granville Barker (1947), and that of Mark Van Doren (1939). All critics note the unsympathetic nature of *Coriolanus*, and many of them pinpoint the difficulty as arising from the lack of soliloquies in the play. As a result we can never get inside his mind. L. C. Knights, in *Some Shakespearean* ***Themes*** (1959), sees that the character is created by "poetic means," but with "subtle psychological probings."

One interesting trend in the characterization of *Coriolanus* lies in the use of modern psychological theories, and David B.

Barron, in "*Coriolanus*: Portrait of the Artist as Infant" (1962), uses the **Sonnets** as well to show neurosis and autobiography in both works. Charles K. Hofling in "An Interpretation of Shakespeare's *Coriolanus*" (1951), applies the theories of Erich Fromm to the central character. Edwin Honig, in "Sejanus and *Coriolanus*: A study in Alienation" (1951), uses a different method, and studies these two characters in terms of their alienation from their "unfilled and ultimately unfulfillable functions as leaders" rather than in a modern psychological manner.

Other critics look at *Coriolanus* through his relationship with Volumnia, and I. R. Browning in "Coriolanus: Boy of Tears" (1958) sees him forever a "mother's boy." Oscar J. Campbell in *Shakespeare's* ***Satire*** (1943) draws attention to aspects of the chastised urchin who fears his mother's wrath and is therefore a figure of satiric derision. F. H. Rouda, however, sees "*Coriolanus* [as] - a Tragedy of Youth" (1961). Both G. Wilson Knight in *The Imperial* ***Theme*** (1951), and John Palmer in *Political Characters of Shakespeare* (1945) emphasize the relationship between mother and son, but Knight, more than most critics, blames Volumnia for her son's limited vision of honor.

It is this rigid attention to honor which makes him what Millar MacLure terms "...the Lonely Dragon" (1955), while William R. Bowden includes him in "The 'Unco Guid' and Shakespeare's *Coriolanus*" (1962). He is really too noble to exist in society. But as Paul Jorgensen notes in *Shakespeare's Military World* (1956), his intense individualism in war makes it impossible for him to move from battlefield to council chamber. In general, the critics unite in deciding that the tragedy of Coriolanus lies in his pride and self-ignorance, and while Volumnia is praised for her Romanness, Oscar Campbell and D. J. Enright note her essentially unfeeling nature, while Harold C. Goddard in *The Meaning of Shakespeare* (1951), sees her as "a liability to any boy." Stopford Brooke, however, sees her as always loving him, and he her. Their love is, as a result, central to the tragedy.

We have incidental character studies of Menenius and Aufidius distributed through most of the critical works already mentioned, but one unexpected study remains. This is J. Middleton Murry's "A Neglected Heroine of Shakespeare" (1921), a sensitive account of the almost wordless Virgilia. In general, however, the character studies center on *Coriolanus* himself and deal only incidentally with the other persons of the play.

RECENT TRENDS

Probably the best evaluative account of twentieth-century trends and fashions in criticism of *Coriolanus* and of the Roman plays in general is to be found in J. C. Maxwell's "Shakespeare's Roman Plays: 1900-1956," in *Shakespeare Survey*, X (1957), 1-11. This article is a summary of the major books and articles issued during those years, with bibliographical and critical detail. It is an invaluable aid to the student.

Some of the more recent criticism has discussed the nature of the play itself. Oscar Campbell, for instance, sees the play as a dramatic satire rather than a tragedy. In attempting to explain the difference between *Coriolanus* and the other Shakespearean heroes he sees the purpose of the plays as the satirizing of a strong man in his folly. D. J. Enright also raised an anti-tragic voice to argue that the play "has certain qualities of an intellectual debate" rather than anything else. What tragedy there is belongs to Rome rather than to *Coriolanus*, and the **theme** of the play is one in which each of the opposing sides understands the other, but neither has self-knowledge.

Derek A. Traversi in *An Approach to Shakespeare* (1938 and rep.) sums up a great deal of critical opinion and sees the tragedy of *Coriolanus* to be one of a futile life. He notes the difference between this play and Shakespeare's other tragedies, but unlike many other critics he does not consider it any worse as a result, only different in emphasis. Few critics have gone so far as to agree with T. S. Eliot in "*Hamlet* and His Problems" (1919) that "it is, along with *Antony and Cleopatra*, Shakespeare's most assured artistic success."

CORIOLANUS

ESSAY QUESTIONS AND ANSWERS

Some of the more important questions raised about the play deserve closer and more specific treatment than that given so far. They may be stated in the following terms:

Why is Coriolanus a cold and unsympathetic hero?

What is Coriolanus' concept of honor?

Why is Coriolanus so successful as a soldier and so unsuccessful as a politician?

What is the greatest virtue of Coriolanus, and what is his greatest vice?

Is Coriolanus a traitor?

By returning to the Volscians does Coriolanus actually seek his own death?

What is the relationship between Volumnia and Coriolanus?

What seems to be the ideal of Roman womanhood expressed in this play?

What is the function of Menenius?

What is the function of the tribunes?

What does Shakespeare mean by democracy in this play, and is he anti-democratic?

What is the function of Aufidius?

What is meant by the so-called "Roman" atmosphere of *Coriolanus?*

Is the conclusion of the play intellectually and emotionally satisfying?

Question: Why is Coriolanus a cold and unsympathetic hero?

Answer: The chief reason for Coriolanus' apparent coldness and lack of sympathy is to be found in the way Shakespeare has built up his character. Unlike most other Shakespearean tragic heroes he has only one notable soliloquy, just before he goes to the house of Aufidius. As a result we do not know exactly what is going through Coriolanus' mind and only see what he says or does in a public situation. Consequently he is difficult to identify with, since we do not understand his emotions.

When Coriolanus does speak he is very often berating someone. He is at his best when he is engaged in insult and has a fine collection of animal epithets which show his great skill in the rhetoric of anger. In fact Coriolanus spends most of the play in a situation of anger. He begins in anger against the

Roman citizens, but then works out his anger in an acceptable military manner on the enemies of Rome at Corioli. However, he castigates his soldiers for their apparent cowardice. After that he is brusque in triumph, grudging in his appeal for the people's voices, and again angry when approval of his appointment as consul is revoked. The act culminates in a tremendous outburst of anger and invective directed against the people of Rome. Throughout the fourth act his anger at Rome continues, while the last act culminates in anger directed against the Volscians, which leads to his death.

On only two occasions does Coriolanus show that he possesses emotions, and these both concern his wife and mother. The first comes in Act IV, when he is leaving Rome for the last time. Then he unselfishly attempts to cheer up his family and friends. The second occasion is the scene of intercession in Act V, when Coriolanus is cut to the heart by the sight of his weeping wife and his kneeling mother. But apart from these two incidents, Coriolanus seems totally self-sufficient and perfectly well aware of what he is doing. And Shakespeare has taken unusual pains to show us both sides of his character so that he appears to be an extraordinary mixture of noble virtues and stubborn blindness. As a result our reactions to him are always qualified.

Above all else, Coriolanus is proud, and with his pride and self-sufficiency goes a total certainty in action. Consequently we have little sympathy with him because of his austere self-righteousness and self-satisfaction. There is really no conflict in his heart as with normal people, and when he is banished we know that in some measure he deserved the treatment he received. Yet at the end of the play, when he is treacherously killed, though we know that the has partly contributed to his death by his speedy and irrational anger, we nevertheless feel that he deserved much better than to suffer such a fate.

As a character Coriolanus is drawn with the mind, not the heart, with emphasis on intellectual and ethical truth rather than emotional truth. Therefore we respect, at times admire, and frequently dislike the character of Coriolanus, but we are never given the opportunity to identify with him, to feel sorry for him, or to love him.

Question: What is Coriolanus' concept of honor?

Answer: Coriolanus' concept of honor is very limited indeed, and it springs largely from Volumnia's teachings. Basically it is a pride in doing his duty, and a pride in personal consistency of behavior. The ideal is always one of individual conduct. Honor to Coriolanus consists of never flinching in the face of danger, of always having the confidence to follow a straight and unwavering course, whatever the consequences. This ideal requires total fearlessness in situations both of war and of peace. Such a concept, allied with personal pride, means that Coriolanus also has contempt for all normal mortals who cannot follow the same harsh and austere code.

This view of honor encompasses no larger issue than personal pride and satisfaction in the doing of duty, and since Coriolanus considers himself better than other human beings, then more is expected of him in the way of duty. Consequently, the motives for his valiant and noble military acts include nothing so unselfish as love of country. Since this honor is totally a personal thing, Coriolanus is very vulnerable to insult because he has no reserves. If his honor is impugned, his entire existence and his certitude are both threatened. He then must retaliate in the only way he understands - he demands satisfaction, not in the formal Renaissance manner of a duel, but instead in the more primitive manner of the vendetta. He fights immediately, or else he tries to gain his own personal vengeance. Nevertheless, he never resorts to anything underhanded; he always acts openly.

Question: Why is Coriolanus so successful as a soldier and so unsuccessful as a politician?

Answer: Coriolanus has really been brought up solely as a warrior and his chief advantages and virtues are those which are best suited to a war situation and are totally unsuited to peace. Duty, boldness, certainty, speed in making decisions, a quick temper, and the ability to hate are all good soldierly virtues which Coriolanus has in abundance. In addition, he also has physical skill in the use of weapons so that he is a brilliant warrior, and in fact he is at his best in situations of destruction rather than administration. He needs free-lance military assignments which test his soldierly initiative, for he is really an expert tradesman, and his trade is war. Action is what a battle situation requires, not diplomacy; the only diplomatic language Coriolanus either knows or understands is to be found in his sword. He has the gift of invective, but not that of soft speech, and his harangue to his frightened men is exactly that of a tough First Sergeant.

On his return to Rome, however, Coriolanus is in a totally strange situation. He cannot bullock his way through opposition; he must be prepared to compromise, to convince, to bend, and at times to give way. None of these courses is really possible within the limits of his stern code of action. He despises the common people, partly because of his experience in war, but he cannot flatter where he does not respect, or simulate interest in the welfare of those whom he hates. Obviously he believes that any outward show of humility and love is dishonest when the mind does not accept it; therefore he refuses to compromise with the people. The only person to whom Coriolanus pays compliments is Aufidius, whose valor he respects, and the only people he loves are Volumnia, Virgilia, and in a different way, Menenius and Cominius, whose common sense and military virtue he admires.

Coriolanus cannot see the difference between the situations of war and those of peace. In war his course was clear, and he expects it to be the same in peace, not realizing that his tactics should be, indeed must be, totally different. Force is useless in politics, and guile is everything; but Coriolanus is too honest and too noble to use guile. We must respect him for this attitude, though at the same time we must pity him for not understanding the expedient principles of peacetime existence. We hate to say that the end justifies the means, but we know that had Coriolanus been more pliable in a worthy cause he might have kept his principles intact and saved his life for the good of Rome.

Question: What is the greatest virtue of Coriolanus and what is his greatest vice?

Answer: This is really two questions in one, but the answer is one word - pride. Almost every action taken by Coriolanus in the course of the play arises from his pride and his ignorance of himself. His blindness in the treatment of others is basically the result of his own self-satisfaction with an immature code of honor that does not see beyond the concept of self. He cannot see that he can be wrong, and acts accordingly. In addition, he cannot see more than one course of action at a time because, with his singleminded, narrow, proud concept of honor and duty, there can be only right and wrong, no middle route. Even Coriolanus' defection to the Volscians is motivated by pride, because when his honor is questioned his pride demands satisfaction, in other words, personal vengeance on Rome.

Question: Is Coriolanus a traitor?

Answer: In his own opinion Coriolanus is not a traitor, and again the reason behind this attitude is his pride. When he goes to the Volscians he is looking out for his own personal revenge on the entire population of Rome because he was banished by all, patricians included. Actually, Coriolanus considers that since his city has banished him he owes it no allegiance, and indeed is a man without a country. Consequently, all that he has is his own personal integrity, and that demands satisfaction. Admittedly this is a fine point, but it is about the only explanation which fits the otherwise consistent behavior of Coriolanus.

Is he then a traitor to the Volscians when he spares Rome? This point is an even more difficult one to answer. Certainly Coriolanus manages to talk himself out of thinking himself a traitor when he spares Rome. For the first time he has discovered that there can be two honorable courses of action, and he is forced into a choice. He looks at the larger issue and sees that he owes a higher loyalty to his family and to Rome than he does to the Volscians. In this situation his choice is emotionally right, but is it morally right in terms of the Volscians?

Coriolanus adopts an unexpectedly subtle argument to prove that he has not acted traitorously to the Volscians, and in returning to Antium to present his case to his employers he is acting honorably. He claims that the Volscians have obtained the moral satisfaction of humiliating Rome, though not the destructive satisfaction of sacking the city. Therefore, he says, the Volscians ought to be happy, and since he, Coriolanus, has managed to "frame convenient peace" without any casualties the expedition ought to be considered a success. Once again the argument is specious. Coriolanus was engaged as a mercenary, in effect under contract to capture Rome, but in simply shaming the city he expects the intangibles of defeat to make amends to the Volscians for his failure to make expenses out of the expedition. His employers had been depending on the booty from Rome to pay the troops, and now they have been run into debt. This is the argument that Aufidius and the lords use when they finally charge Coriolanus with treason. Yet in one sense Coriolanus is right; he has managed to fulfill the conditions of his employment by bringing Rome to, her knees.

At no time does Coriolanus see himself as a traitor, the one charge that is guaranteed to enrage him. Consequently when Aufidius repeats the insult he had first heard from Sicinius in Rome, he reacts in exactly the same way. Coriolanus' honor is challenged, and in his customary immature rage he demands satisfaction and is killed ignominiously, though his death in part expiates his defection from the Volscian cause.

Question: By returning to the Volscians does Coriolanus actually seek his own death?

Answer: In a sense Coriolanus does seek his death, because after acceding to his mother's pleas, he remarks that she has won a happy victory for Rome, but one that is most mortal, or fatal, for him. This is indeed the case, for now he has nowhere to go. He cannot live in Rome, nor can he live on among the Volscians after betraying some of the terms of his employment contract. His argument that he has won a moral victory is really an attempt to put the best face on the matter. But throughout the play Coriolanus has never flinched in the face of danger, especially where his honor is involved. At this moment he is duty bound, or honor bound, to return to Antium to give an account of the expedition. He is almost certain that his return will cause his death, but he must go. Unfortunately, as is customary with him, he mars the effect of his act by his own pride, foolishness, and rage.

Question: What is the relationship between Volumnia and Coriolanus?

Answer: Volumnia is a widow who had had to bring up her only son alone. As a result, in trying to avoid rearing Coriolanus as a weakling she has gone to the opposite extreme. At the very beginning of the play (I.iii) she tells of her joy in his military prowess and explains the way she sent him to the "cruel war" when he was a mere boy. She glories in his wounds and is extraordinarily ambitious for him both militarily and politically.

Her aim seems to have been to make him into her image of a perfect Roman citizen, and in the process she has made him a reflection of herself in staunchness, valor, and attention to personal honor. His pride, however, she refuses to admit as coming from her, because she is more politic in her approaches and can bend where Coriolanus refuses to do so. The chief bond between mother and son seems to be a joint pride in military achievements. Coriolanus does his bold deeds partly to please his mother, and her approval means more to him than almost anything else. He can put up with opprobrium from the people and hatred from the enemy, but he must on all occasions gain and keep his mother's approval.

In that respect their relationship is most unusual, because Volumnia continues to be the touchstone of behavior for her son. As a result he is quite horrified when she suggests that he humble himself, because she seems to be negating the lessons she has taught him. Her contempt speedily brings him round, as it also does in the fifth act. Volumnia is Rome and the epitome of Roman virtues for Coriolanus, and therefore when she appears to reject him she has in effect told him that he has failed in following the only code of behavior he knows and understands.

Lastly, how much love is there between Coriolanus and his mother? Their love is of a peculiarly active, yet unspoken kind. Coriolanus must demonstrate his affection by deeds, not words, and similarly, Volumnia seems to be a woman who has deliberately avoided the open shows of feminine affection in order to make her son a better warrior. They understand each other very well, they even seem to speak roughly to each other. But at the end of the play Volumnia teaches Coriolanus by example the one lesson she had apparently overlooked - the lesson of looking beyond himself. She is prepared to sacrifice him for Rome, and therefore he should be prepared to sacrifice himself for both her and Rome. As before, she has taught him to be totally Roman, and he follows her, his mother, in this ideal, as he always has. The motivation is, I believe, love, but a love that is implied rather than actually spoken, and a love that is tempered by a stern code of honor.

Question: What seems to be the ideal of Roman womanhood expressed in this play?

Answer: The ideal of Roman womanhood shown in this play is a three-fold one. First we have the staunch Roman matron, Volumnia, who will sacrifice everything for her loyalty to Rome, even at the risk of breaking her own heart. Secondly we have the ideal of domestic virtues in Virgilia, the wife, who is soft, gentle, loving, and retiring. Thirdly, in Valeria we have the merry lady who is charming and beautiful, and also noted for her unassailable virtue and chastity. Each of these three women is shown as altogether admirable in her own way.

Question: What is the function of Menenius?

Answer: Menenius is extremely important in the play and he is almost totally original with Shakespeare who created him out of a hint in Plutarch. His task is to present the moderate aristocratic point of view in the play. His celebrated tale of the belly and the members, for instance, is a plea for aristocratic centralized government and the status quo. He states both the rights and duties of all members of the commonwealth, though he makes his own position perfectly clear. He believes that nobles are the naturally ordained rulers of the lesser common people, and he says so, but with such humor that the plebeians accept his comments in good humor.

He is always opposed to the tribunes, and the supporter of Coriolanus, whom he loves as a son. In addition, he sees himself as the potential savior of Rome when he goes to plead with Coriolanus. On all occasions he pleads, though sometimes ineffectually, for moderation in behavior, but he does not favor peace and quiet at any price. He wants reason to be observed on all occasions, and the only reasonable solution he can ever see is a conservative approach in which the aristocracy rules. He has an easy air of authority and superiority and as a result manages to get along well with the plebeians who trust him. He is really the ideal kind of aristocrat.

Question: What is the function of the tribunes?

Answer: Shakespeare has given the tribunes more justification than did Plutarch by showing more of the legitimate grievances of the plebeians, and also by omitting one insurrection instigated almost irresponsibly by the tribunes. They are the voice of the common people, but their honesty is always suspect. Are they working for themselves and their own position, or for the good of the state?

The tribunes are directly opposed to Menenius and Coriolanus, but it is the latter whom they really hate. Actually they do have some right on their side, because Coriolanus does hate the plebeians, and consequently the tribunes ought to veto his appointment. It is the manner of their opposition that makes them seem so unsavory. Politically speaking, the tribunes are much cleverer than anyone else in the play. They know exactly how to manipulate a situation to their own advantage and they make use of demagogic tactics to make their point and influence their followers. When they are in command of the action they speedily overreach themselves and move toward a kind of dictatorship of the mob. The injustice of the sentence of death or banishment on Coriolanus is obvious because he is not given a fair trial, being denied the right to speak in his own defense until Sicinius has enraged him.

Then, when the tribunes have their way, they receive the gratitude of the people almost like patricians in their secretly contemptuous attitude toward the common folk. Their motives may have been laudable at first, but eventually they seem to be corrupted by power. In the tribunes Shakespeare shows the operations of so-called practical politicians and also the dangers of divided control in a country.

Question: What does Shakespeare mean by democracy in this play, and is he anti-democratic?

Answer: Democracy in *Coriolanus* is not representative government complete with checks and balances as we know the term today. To the orthodox political thinkers and writers of Shakespeare's day it was something to be avoided because it meant unbridled rule by the many. Aristotle, in the *Ethics*, thought that democracy meant total equality for all, with consequent license for all kinds of behavior. He saw democracy as a deviation from something that was not evil-timocracy-which meant equality of citizens with liberty to seek only the good. What Shakespeare really shows us in this play is therefore the horror of mob rule and the political and moral chaos that it causes. He is not, as a result, anti-democratic in the modern sense of the word, but for him and for other orthodox political thinkers of his day, the overthrow of a central authority was unthinkable because a monarch was God's representative on earth and his power was ordained by divine right.

Question: What is the function of Aufidius?

Answer: Aufidius is, of course, a foil character to Coriolanus. As a result he is used to show up the innate nobility and valor of his enemy. Shakespeare makes him a lesser man, but not too much less than Coriolanus, for in more political respects Aufidius is a shrewder person than the Roman. On occasion Aufidius can outdo Coriolanus in generosity, but at times he is more given to jealousy and is more smallminded, stooping to conspiracy and underhanded plotting to gain his ends.

In some respects Shakespeare has increased the importance of the character of Aufidius by using him to display Coriolanus' military skill at the beginning of the play. But at the same time he has confused the issue by making Aufidius so much the operative figure in the destruction of Coriolanus. As a result the contradiction is not fully resolved between his nobility, valor and generosity towards a former enemy, and his conspiratorial plotting and smallminded jealousy earlier in the play. In this respect Shakespeare may have overloaded his character by giving him too much to do. Perhaps the funeral oration is an example of this fault, yet the tribute from a dangerous enemy is doubly important because of its source.

Question: What is meant by the so-called "Roman" atmosphere of *Coriolanus?*

Answer: In general what is meant is the austerity of the entire play with its insistence on the intellect rather than the emotions. The Romans were traditionally considered to be devoted to the pursuit of nobility, the good of their city, and the preservation of law and order, at the expense of the individual if necessary. The "classical temper" of *Coriolanus* is most notably to be found in the deliberate avoidance of emotional effects in poetry and **imagery**, as well as in character drawing. The relationships among the characters of the play are likewise carefully controlled. In fact control is one of the key words of the play. Shakespeare seems to have deliberately disciplined his art to appeal to the mind. This emphasis can best be appreciated by comparing *Coriolanus* with the play which immediately preceded it, *Antony and Cleopatra*. In some respects Shakespeare has made of *Coriolanus* a political debate and it is the most avowedly political of his works. At the same time he has managed to embody political principles in realistically drawn characters so that it is hard to detach the stern political attitudes from the equally stern and uncompromising characters. Rome's attributes are hard and they do not respect the emotions of the individual, and that is the "Roman" atmosphere that Shakespeare manages to convey.

Question: Is the conclusion of the play intellectually and emotionally satisfying?

Answer: The end of *Coriolanus* is more satisfying intellectually than emotionally. The reason is that we have never been able fully to identify with Coriolanus because he is a man without an inner conflict, until Act V. Then, when he has resolved the conflict between mercy and honor, which Aufidius perceives so well, he has violated his somewhat narrow moral and intellectual integrity, and he must die. This fact is intellectually inevitable, but the emotional inevitability never comes through in the same way that it does in King Lear, for instance. There, the old king has reached the end of his life and has learned; indeed the act of his learning is the spiritual culmination of his existence. Also, if one believes that he dies of joy thinking that Cordelia lives, then he dies on a note of triumph.

With Coriolanus, however, there is no triumph in his death, and no joy in his moment of enlightenment. He has had immense potential for noble and good acts, but he has willfully and foolishly thrown away his chances. He is indeed noble, and he proves this fact by his discovery of his larger loyalty to Rome and his subsequent return to Antium. But then he bridles at a cheap insult and replies in kind. He is again the immature young man, enraged because someone has affronted him, and in what is almost a tantrum he defies everyone present. In reply to Aufidius' scornful "boy of tears" he draws his sword to lash out in a futile gesture of rage, and he is killed by a group of conspirators.

This death is a waste in terms of spiritual advancement, and it is intellectually ironic that after his enlightenment Coriolanus should be so destroyed by his pre-existing faults. As a result, the dominant feeling at the conclusion of the play is that the hero acted rightly in sparing Rome, but that he did in some way deserve the death that came upon him. Emotionally, however, we are not satisfied, because the death of Coriolanus is so much less noble than the man's nature, and because it sums up the ultimate futility and waste that made up his life.

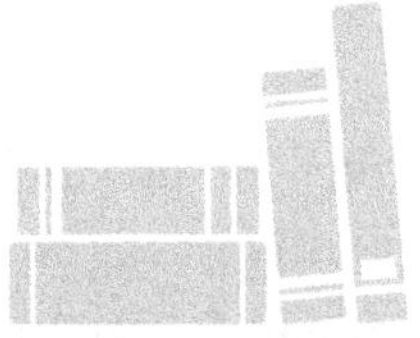

BIBLIOGRAPHY

SHAKESPEARE BIOGRAPHY

Bentley, G. E. *Shakespeare: A Biographical Handbook.* New Haven: Yale University Press, 1961.

Chambers, E. K. *William Shakespeare: A Study of Facts and Problems.* Oxford: Clarendon Press, 1930. 2 vols.

Chute, Marchette. *Shakespeare of London.* New York: E. P. Dutton, 1949.

Halliday, F. E. *The Life of Shakespeare.* London: Duckworth, 1961.

Parrott, Thomas Marc. *William Shakespeare: A Handbook.* Rev. ed. New York: Scribner's, 1955.

Wright, Louis B. *Shakespeare for Everyman.* New York: Washington Square Press, 1964.

THE THEATRE

Adams, John Cranford. *The Globe Playhouse.* Cambridge [Mass.]: Harvard University Press, 1943.

Baldwin, T. W. *The Organization and Personnel of the Shakespearean Company.* Princeton: Princeton University Press, 1927.

Beckerman, Bernard. *Shakespeare at the Globe.* New York: Macmillan, 1962.

Bentley, G. E. "Shakespeare and the Blackfriars Theatre." *Shakespeare Survey,* I (1948), 38-50.

Chambers, E. K. *The Elizabethan stage.* Oxford: Clarendon Press, 1923. 4 vols.

Harbage, Alfred. *Shakespeare and the Rival Traditions.* New York: Macmillan, 1952.

Harbage, Alfred. *Shakespeare's Audience.* New York: Columbia University Press, 1941.

Hodges, C. Walter. *The Globe Restored.* New York: Coward McCann, 1953.

Hosley, Richard. "The Discovery-Space in Shakespeare's Globe." *Shakespeare Survey,* XII (1959), 35-46.

Hosley, Richard. "The Gallery over the Stage in the Public Playhouse of Shakespeare's Time." *Shakespeare Quarterly,* VIII (1955), 15-31.

Hosley, Richard. "Shakespeare's Use of a Gallery over the Stage." *Shakespeare Survey,* X (1957), 77-89.

Hotson, J. Leslie. *Shakespeare's* "Wooden O-letter." London: Macmillan, 1960.

Lawrence, W. J. *The Physical Conditions of the Elizabethan Public Playhouse.* Cambridge [Mass.]: Harvard University Press, 1927.

Nagler, Alois M. *Shakespeare's Stage.* New Haven: Yale University Press, 1958.

Smith, Irwin. *Shakespeare's Globe Playhouse*. New York: Scribner's, 1956.

SOURCES AND BACKGROUND

Barroll, J. Leeds." Shakespeare and Roman History." *Modern Language Review*, LIII (1958), 327-343.

Case, R. H., ed. *The Tragedy of Coriolanus*. "Arden Edition." London: Methuen, 1922.

Chappell, Fred. "Shakespeare's *Coriolanus* and Plutarch's life of Cato." *Renaissance Papers*, No. 914 (1962), pp. 9-16.

Heuer, Hermann. "From Plutarch to Shakespeare: A Study of *Coriolanus*." *Shakespeare Survey*, X (1957), 50-59.

Jorgensen, Paul A. "Shakespeare's *Coriolanus*: An Elizabethan Soldier." *PMLA*, LXIV (1949), 221-235.

Jorgensen, Paul A. *Shakespeare's Military World*. Berkeley and Los Angeles: University of California Press, 1956.

Lees, F. N. "*Coriolanus*, Aristotle, and Bacon." *Review of English Studies*, n. s. I (Ap. 1950), 114-125.

MacCallum, M. W. *Shakespeare's Roman Plays and Their Background*. London: Macmillan, 1910.

Maxwell, J. C. "Menenius' Fable." *Notes and Queries*, Vol. 198, No. 8 (Aug. 1953), p. 329.

Muir, Kenneth. The Background of *Coriolanus*." *Shakespeare Quarterly*, X (1959), 137-145.

Muir, Kenneth. "Menenius' Fable." *Notes and Queries*, Vol. 198, No. 6 (Jun. 1953), pp. 240-242.

Pettet, E. C. "*Coriolanus* and the Midlands Insurrection of 1607." *Shakespeare Survey*, III (1950), 34-42.

Phillips, James E., Jr. *The State in Shakespeare's Greek and Roman Plays*. New York: Columbia University Press, 1940.

Shanker, Sidney. "Some Clues for *Coriolanus.*" *Shakespeare Association Bulletin*, XXIV (1949), 209-213.

Spencer, T. J. B. "Shakespeare and the Elizabethan Romans." *Shakespeare Survey*, X (1957), 27-38.

Spencer, T. J. B., ed. *Shakespeare's Plutarch*. London: Penguin Books, 1964.

Wilson, J. Dover, ed. *The Tragedy of Coriolanus*. "New Shakespeare." Cambridge: Cambridge University Press. 1960.

Zeeveld, W. Gordon. "*Coriolanus* and Jacobean Politics." *Modern Language Review*, LVII (1962), 321-334.

CRITICISM: TEXTUAL AND INTERPRETIVE

Barker, Harley Granville. *Prefaces to Shakespeare*. Princeton: Princeton University Press, 1947. Vol. II.

Barron, David B. "*Coriolanus*: Portrait of the Artist as Infant." *American Imago*, XIX (1962), 171-193.

Bowden, William R. "The 'Unco Guid' and Shakespeare's *Coriolanus.*" *Shakespeare Quarterly*, XIII (1962), 41-48.

Bradley, A. C. "*Coriolanus.*" *British Academy Shakespeare Lecture*, 1912. Reprinted in *A Miscellany*. London: Macmillan, 1929.

Bradley, A. C. *Shakespearean Tragedy*. London: Macmillan, 1904.

Brandes, Georg. *William Shakespeare: A Critical Study*, trans. William Archer and others. London: Heinemann, 1920. [Orig. pub. 1898.]

Brooke, Stopford. *On Ten Plays of Shakespeare*. London: Constable, 1905.

Brown, Huntington. "Enter the Shakespearean Tragic Hero." *Essays in Criticism*, III (1953), 285-302.

Browning, I. R. "*Coriolanus*: Boy of Tears." *Essays in Criticism*, V (1955), 18-31.

Campbell, Oscar James. *Shakespeare's **Satire***. New York: Oxford University Press, 1943.

Chambers, E. K. *Shakespeare: A Survey*. New York: Hill and Wang, Dramabook, n.d. [Orig. pub. 1925.]

Charney, Maurice, ed. *Discussions of Shakespeare's Roman Plays*. Boston: D. C. Heath, 1964.

Charney, Maurice. "The **Imagery** of Food and Eating in *Coriolanus.*" *Essays in Literary History*, XVI (1961), 37-55.

Charney, Maurice. *Shakespeare's Roman Plays: The Function of Imagery in the Drama*. Cambridge [Mass.]: Harvard University Press, 1961.

Clemen, Wolfgang H. *The Development of Shakespeare's **Imagery***. Cambridge [Mass.]: Harvard University Press, 1951.

Dean, Leonard F. "Voice and Deed in *Coriolanus*." *University of Kansas City Review*, XXI (1955), 177-184.

Dennis, John. *An Essay on the Genius and Writings of Shakespeare* (1712). See Eastman and Harrison.

Dowden, Edward. *Shakespeare: A Critical Study of His Mind and Art*. New York and London: Harper, 1905.

Draper, John W. "Political **Themes** in Shakespeare's Later Plays." *Journal of English and Germanic Philology*, XXV (1936), 61-93.

Eastman, A. M., and G. B. Harrison, eds. *Shakespeare's Critics from Jonson to Auden: A Medley of Judgments*. Ann Arbor: University of Michigan Press, 1964.

Eliot, T. S. "*Hamlet* and His Problems" (1919), in *Selected Essays*. New York: Harcourt, Brace, 1950.

Enright, D. J. "*Coriolanus*: Tragedy or Debate?" *Essays in Criticism*, IV (1954), 1-19.

Evans, B. Ifor. *The Language of Shakespeare's Plays*. London: Methuen, 1951.

Farnham, Willard. *Shakespeare's Tragic Frontier*. Berkeley and Los Angeles: University of California Press, 1950.

Goddard, Harold C. *The Meaning of Shakespeare*. Chicago: University of Chicago Press, 1951.

Hazlitt, William. *Characters of Shakespeare's Plays* (1817) See Eastman and Harrison.

Hofling, Charles K. "An Interpretation of Shakespeare's *Coriolanus*." *American Imago*, XIV (1957), 407-435.

Honig, Edwin. "Sejanus and *Coriolanus*: A Study in Alienation." *Modern Language Quarterly*, XII (1951), 407-421.

Hunter, G. K. "Shakespeare's Hydra." *Notes and Queries*, Vol. 198, No. 3 (Mar. 1953), pp. 100-101.

Johnson, Samuel. *Samuel Johnson on Shakespeare*, ed. W. K. Wimsatt, Jr. New York: Hill and Wang, Dramabook, 1960.

Jorgensen, Paul A. "Divided Command in Shakespeare." *PMLA*, LXX (1955), 750-761.

Kirschbaum, Leo. "Shakespeare's Stage Blood and Its Critical Significance." *PMLA*, LXIV (1949), 517-529.

Knights, L. C. "Shakespeare and Political Wisdom: A Note on the Personalism of *Julius Caesar* and *Coriolanus*." *Sewanee Review*, LXI (1953), 43-55.

MacLure, Millar. "Shakespeare and the Lonely Dragon." *University of Toronto Quarterly*, XXIV (1955), 109-120.

Maxwell, J. C. "Animal **Imagery** in *Coriolanus*." *Modern Language Review*, XLII (1947), 417-421.

Maxwell, J. C. "Shakespeare's Roman Plays: 1900-1956." *Shakespeare Survey*, X (1957), 1-11.

Murry, John Middleton. "*Coriolanus*" (1922). Reprinted in *Discoveries*. London: Collins, 1924.

Oliver, H. J. "*Coriolanus* as Tragic Hero." *Shakespeare Quarterly*, X (1959), 53-60.

Palmer, John. *Political Characters of Shakespeare*. London: Macmillan, 1945.

Proser, Matthew. "*Coriolanus*: The Constant Warrior and the State." *College English*, XXIV (1963), 507-512.

Ribner, Irving. "The Tragedy of *Coriolanus*." *English Studies*, XXXIV (1953), 1-9.

Roth, R. "Another World of Shakespeare." *Modern Philology*, XLIX (1951-52), 42-61.

Rouda, F. H. "*Coriolanus* - A Tragedy of Youth." *Shakespeare Quarterly*, XII (1961), 103-106.

Schlosser, Anselm. "Reflections upon Shakespeare's *Coriolanus*." *Philologica Pragensia*, VI (1963), 11-21

Sen, Sailendra Kumar. "What Happens in *Coriolanus*." *Shakespeare Quarterly*, IX (1958), 331-345.

Smith, Gordon Ross. "Authoritarian Patterns in Shakespeare's *Coriolanus*." *Literature and Psychology*, IX (1959), 45-51.

Spurgeon, Caroline. *Shakespeare's* ***Imagery*** *and What It Tells Us*. Cambridge: Cambridge University Press, 1935.

Stauffer, Donald. *Shakespeare's World of Images*. New York: Norton, 1949.

Stirling, Brents. *The Populace in Shakespeare*. New York: Columbia University Press, 1949.

Swinburne, A. C. *A Study of Shakespeare* (1880). See Eastman and Harrison.

Tanselle, G. Thomas, and Florence W. Dunbar. "Legal Language in *Coriolanus*." *Shakespeare Quarterly*, XIII (1962), 231-238.

Traversi, Derek A. *An Approach to Shakespeare*. 2nd ed. rev. and enl. Garden City, New York: Doubleday, 1956.

Van Doren, Mark. *Shakespeare*. New York: Holt, 1939.

Walker, Roy. "The Northern Star: An Essay on the Roman Plays." *Shakespeare Quarterly*, II (1951), 287-293.

www.ingramcontent.com/pod-product-compliance
Lightning Source LLC
Chambersburg PA
CBHW061507050726
47593CB00002B/489

* 9 7 8 1 6 4 5 4 2 5 5 6 4 *